The Chicago Handbook for **Teacher**

CHICAGO GUIDES TO ACADEMIC LIFE

THE CHICAGO HANDBOOK FOR

Teachers

A Practical Guide to the College Classroom Second Edition

ALAN BRINKLEY, ESAM EL-FAKAHANY, BETTY DESSANTS,

MICHAEL FLAMM, CHARLES B. FORCEY, JR., MATHEW L. OUELLETT,

AND ERIC ROTHSCHILD

The University of Chicago Press

Chicago and London

The University of Chicago Press, Chicago 60637
The University of Chicago Press, Ltd., London
© 2011 by The University of Chicago
All rights reserved. Published 2011
Printed in the United States of America

20 19 18 17 16 15 14 13 12 11   1 2 3 4 5

ISBN-13: 978-0-226-07527-3 (cloth)
ISBN-10: 0-226-07527-3 (cloth)
ISBN-13: 978-0-226-07528-0 (paper)
ISBN-10: 0-226-07528-1 (paper)

Library of Congress Cataloging-in-Publication Data
The Chicago handbook for teachers : a practical guide to the college classroom / Alan
    Brinkley . . . [et al.]. — 2nd ed.
        p. cm. — (Chicago guides to academic life)
    Includes index.
    ISBN-13: 978-0-226-07527-3 (cloth: alk. paper)
    ISBN-10: 0-226-07527-3 (cloth: alk. paper)
    ISBN-13: 978-0-226-07528-0 (pbk.: alk. paper)
    ISBN-10: 0-226-07528-1 (pbk.: alk. paper)
    1. College teaching—Handbooks, manuals, etc. 2. College teachers—Handbooks,
    manuals, etc. I. Brinkley, Alan.
    LB2331.C52332 2011
    378.1'25—dc22

                                                            2010032924

Contents

Introduction

This book has a very simple purpose. It is designed to offer practical advice to teachers in college courses—advice on how to navigate many of the most common challenges they are likely to face in and out of the classroom. We expect it to be particularly helpful to beginning teachers, but we believe many experienced teachers will find the book useful and rewarding as well.

The project had its origins in a conversation about teaching at a meeting of the Executive Board of the Organization of American Historians years ago, when two of the authors were members of the board. There was general agreement among the experienced scholars and teachers present that day that most beginning college instructors—graduate students having their first experiences as teaching assistants, new Ph.D.'s starting their first teaching jobs—received little or no training in how to deal with the classroom before they entered it. Primary and secondary public school teachers ordinarily receive teacher training in education schools or departments. College, university, and independent school teachers, by contrast, are usually trained intensively in their disciplines (history, English, economics, physics, and so on), but seldom in the craft of teaching itself. There is a growing, and welcome, movement in many graduate schools to incorporate teacher training into the traditional curriculum. But it remains the case that many, perhaps most, new college and independent school teachers design their courses and enter their classrooms for the first time without very much guidance from anyone. This book was written with them in mind. We call it a "handbook" because, while we think many teachers may wish to read it in its entirety, we believe others may wish to consult it periodically for help in dealing with particular questions or problems.

We do not claim here to present a coherent theory of teaching or learning. There are many such theories, and they are the subject of a large and valuable literature produced by scholars of education and others. Our goal, however, is the simpler one of answering common logistical questions and using our own experiences in the classroom to offer ideas and lessons that we think other teachers might find useful. In eleven relatively brief chapters, we have tried to present practical suggestions for dealing with some of the basic aspects of teaching: designing a course, preparing for the first class, leading a discussion, managing classroom dynamics, delivering a lecture, supervising research and writing, giving and grading exams, evaluating your own teaching, dealing with diversity issues, facing the challenges of teaching science, and making use of new electronic resources.

There are, needless to say, many issues related to teaching that this book does not address, and many ideas, techniques, and innovations for the classroom beyond those we have included. Both new and experienced teachers have many other resources from which they can draw as they try to improve their students—and their own—classroom experiences. We suggest some such resources in our brief bibliography, but there are also many others.

One problem that all teachers face is the problem of time. People outside the academic world often think of college or university teachers as people who live uniquely leisured lives. Those of us who actually work in academia know otherwise. Many of us enjoy more extended vacations than do people in most other professions, it is true. But during the teaching year, we are often compelled to balance an overwhelming number of commitments and responsibilities within a painfully short period of time: teaching classes, advising, grading, serving on committees, commuting, meeting obligations to families and communities, and so forth. Some teachers have very heavy course loads and can find very little time for each of the many preparations demanded of them. Other teachers have part-time jobs, sometimes several of them, and must scramble to find new work even as they are finishing the old. Many college teachers have to balance their teaching obligations against the pressure to do research and to publish, which are often prerequisites to professional survival.

No one will have time to implement all the suggestions in this book—let alone the many other ideas and suggestions available in other sources. Some people will have little time for any of them. We realize, therefore, that our prescriptions for teaching successfully will, in the world most teachers inhabit, need to be balanced against what is possible in pressured and often difficult professional lives.

But teaching is a cumulative art. We learn over time, just as our students do. Things you have no time to try one year may be possible in another. A course that begins shakily may improve after two or three tries, and as you slowly incorporate new methods and techniques into your teaching. You should not be discouraged when the realities of your professional life make it hard to enhance your teaching quickly. Do what you can in the time you have, and over several years—if you keep working at it—your teaching will get better.

Many of the authors of this book are historians, and our common experience in a single discipline has undoubtedly shaped the way we think about teaching. Teachers of English or psychology or chemistry or any other discipline would undoubtedly produce a rather different book. But almost everything we present here is, we believe, applicable to teaching in a wide range of fields—certainly to other disciplines in the humanities and social sciences, much of it also to the natural sciences and to the professional fields.

Teaching, particularly for the first time, can be a lonely and intimidating experience. We hope that the material we present here will make the experience less daunting and more rewarding—both for instructors and for their students.

We thank the many colleagues, friends, and family members who contributed, both directly and indirectly, to this book. Because there are seven authors, the list of people who should be acknowledged is too long to include here, and we hope they will forgive us for not thanking them by name. We are also grateful to John Tryneski and David Morrow of the University of Chicago Press for their help in guiding this project to publication. Finally, we thank our students, who have taught us most of what we know about teaching—and many other things as well.

Getting Ready

Well before your first entrance into the classroom, you will make decisions about your teaching that will shape nearly everything that happens later. The first step in creating a successful course is planning and designing it, a task that often begins months before the start of the term. It may begin with an early request from your library or bookstore for a list of your assigned readings—particularly now that federal law requires instructors to post book lists on the school's Web site before registration. It might begin with a question from the registrar or some other administrator about what kind of classroom space you will need. And it might begin with your department or your prospective students asking for copies of your syllabus. Thinking carefully in advance about how you structure your course is the first step toward successful teaching.

Designing a course is difficult enough without trying to reinvent the wheel. Ask colleagues (in your own institution or in others) to share their materials from similar courses to get an idea of how others have taught the subject. Some departments maintain a file of syllabi for the use of both graduate students and faculty. Check the Internet, where an increasing number of professional organizations, academic departments, and individual instructors have Web pages with syllabi and course outlines.

However useful the ideas of others might be, you must weigh any suggestions you receive against the circumstances of your school and students.

In planning a class, you need to think about three components of course design: (1) deciding what you want your students to learn, (2) choosing effective and appropriate course materials, and (3) creating a clear and informative syllabus.

What Do You Want Your Students to Learn?

This sounds like an obvious question, but it is one to which teachers do not always give sufficient thought. You expect your students to learn something about whatever the subject of your course may be, but what they will learn about those subjects is something to which you should devote considerable thought. You must also think about what you want students to gain in conceptual knowledge and skills, and how you want them to gain it. Whether you are leading a large lecture class, a small research seminar, or something in between, the answers to these questions should help determine everything you do in your course.

One way to think about how to help your students to learn is to develop a series of thematic questions relevant to your discipline and course subject. Such themes, sometimes presented to students as questions, form the underlying structure of the class. You might use these questions on a final exam or as essay assignments that you would like your students to be able to tackle toward the end of the term. Once you have done that, begin thinking about what it will take to get your students to the point where they can do what you expect of them.

Consider carefully what material you wish to present to them: what you want them to read, what kind of research or other independent work you want them to do, what kind of problem sets you wish them to handle, and what you want to discuss in class. The most stimulating book and the most engaging lecture will have little lasting impact on your students if it is not linked to the larger purpose you want your course to serve. The thematic content of a course can be very simple or very complicated; it can be chronological or topical or theoretical or methodological. Whatever it is, it should be reasonably transparent. Make sure you know what you want your students to learn before you assign books and other materials.

Thinking about how to get your students to achieve requires thinking about the way in which you want them to learn. Do you want students to learn to do serious research? If so, you should organize your course so that research is an integral part of it from the beginning. You might, for example, assign a brief and relatively simple paper at the beginning of the term to give students some early research experience. Do you want your course to emphasize writing skills? If so, build in papers from the beginning and establish guidelines, both for your students and for yourself, about how the writing is to be evaluated and how improvement is to be measured. Do you want students to learn how to present ideas and arguments in public? If so, structure student presentations carefully and explain them clearly. Do you want your course to be a collaborative experience? If you do, decide at the start how students are to work together, and organize the course around those decisions.

You may not, of course, have freedom to design a course as you wish. If your course is designed by others, then you will have to plan your course to serve the objectives imposed on you. If you are a graduate student teaching a discussion section or conducting a lab, for example, you will likely be serving a structure created by the supervising professor. Even then, however, you should give serious thought to how you wish to lead your students toward the course's goals, whether the goals are your own or those of others.

Choosing Course Materials

Once you have given some thought to what you want your students to learn, you can begin to think about what materials you can assign to them that will best serve your purposes.

First, think about what you can expect of your students. Think also about the level of your students. If you are teaching an introductory course, your expectations—both for the amount of reading and for the difficulty of it—should be different from those for a course aimed at more advanced students. In a class of mixed levels, ask yourself whom you most want the course to serve and choose materials aimed at them.

Think carefully not just about the level, but also about the quantity of material you assign: how much reading and other work is it realistic to expect students to do? This should reflect the nature and level of your students. It should also reflect the demands placed on them by other courses. If your students are taking five or six courses a term, your expectations for how much they can read or write for you will be lower than if they are taking three or four. Whatever you decide, try to assign roughly the same amount of work each week, with reductions periodically when papers or other projects are due, or when exams are scheduled. If you assign too much reading, your students simply will not do it all, and you will have little control over what they choose to read and what they do not.

Finally, think as well about the cost of the materials you are assigning. Given the escalating prices of books and other media, keep in mind the amount of money you are asking students to spend relative to how much they will use the materials in the course. If you ask students to purchase several books, be sure that you plan to make significant use of them. You should, if possible, place everything you assign on reserve in your institution's library. (Allow sufficient time for the books to get there by your first day of class.) Many libraries offer programs, such as Blackboard or Electronic Reserve, for reserve materials. If your department has its own reading room, you might wish to create an informal reserve shelf of your own, with copies or photocopies of assigned reading available there. An increasing amount of material is available for free on the Internet, and you may wish to augment materials for purchase with Web-based material—including, perhaps, material you yourself decide to place on a Web site—if your students have ready access to the Internet. Check with your institution's library for the availability of databases that provide online resources.

Using Visual and Audio Materials

Books and other published materials are the traditional stuff of teaching, but many other resources are available to you as well—films, audio recordings, computerized audiovisual material, Web sites, class handouts.

Students usually respond well to visual and audio material, and the ready availability of such material in many forms makes their use much easier today than it was in the past. A DVD or a recording can be a diversion. But if you prepare students for what they are going to see, and then engage them in a discussion or a writing exercise afterward, visual and audio material will complement and not distract from written or spoken material.

Visual images are essential to teaching in many fields, for example, art history. But even if you are teaching a course that is not dependent on visual aids, images can be a valuable complement to lectures and discussions. Presentation software, such as Microsoft PowerPoint, has largely replaced slides for classroom use. In addition, many institutions provide the means to convert slides and photographs into PowerPoint images, and many individual teachers now have the equipment—for example, a scanner or a digital camera—needed to convert images to PowerPoint on their own.

You can also create PowerPoint presentations that provide outlines of the text of a lecture, or incorporate graphs, charts, data sheets, cartoons, photos, sketches, diagrams, and maps. Integrating them within your notes or outlines not only enhances your lecture or discussion but also saves you a great deal of time that you might otherwise spend in class writing on the blackboard. PowerPoint, however, is a supplement to successful teaching, not a substitute for it.

Although the initial preparation of a PowerPoint presentation can be time-consuming, it can be can be used again, perhaps with modifications, in the future. As with any teaching material, choose and organize your images carefully, keeping in mind your goals for the particular lesson. Try to include a full bibliographical citation on each image that you did not create yourself.

As professors and students increasingly take advantage of the Internet and Web-based education, you may find prepackaged programs that allow you to supplement your lessons with multimedia presentations accessed directly though Internet sites or on CD-ROMs. Ask at your school's media center or check publishers' catalogues to see if any might suit your needs.

Before you commit yourself to using visual, audio, or computerized materials, make sure that your institution can make the necessary facilities and equipment available to you and that you will know how to use them. It is both embarrassing and disruptive to fumble with technology that does not work or that you do not know how to use. Also make sure that your classroom will be appropriate for the technologies you are using. If you wish to use computerized materials, make sure that you have a room that is equipped for that.

Finding Course Materials

Many resources will help you find materials that might be useful for your teaching. If you are looking for ideas for books to assign, spend some time browsing through the catalogues or Web sites of presses that publish prominently in your field and request books you are considering assigning from a publisher (using a toll-free number or online form). Browsing through bookstores—both the traditional ones and the virtual ones such as Amazon.com—is another valuable way of discovering books you might wish to use. If you attend a large professional conference, publishers will usually be exhibiting their wares. Many research libraries also now offer digital "e-book" versions of published material that students can access on the Internet for free. Most scholarly journals are also now available online through college and university Web sites, but less often in independent school libraries. And ask fellow instructors about books that worked well—or didn't.

Once you have an idea of what books you might want to use, check in the current Books in Print on the Internet or in Web-based booksellers for information about what is in print, what is in paperback, and what things cost. The online bookstores have the additional advantage of being places from which your students can order books if they are not available in the campus bookstore or if they are not discounted there.

Some books are published simultaneously in "trade" editions (which are sold in ordinary bookstores) and "college editions" (which are sold through the publisher's sales representatives and are ordered by instructors). Check to see which is the less expensive. Publishers sometimes package texts with supplementary printed and audiovisual materials for students and instructors and sell them at reduced prices for the entire package. If you are ordering a textbook, check to see what materials are available to you and your students along with it and what you need to do to get them. Large college publishers ordinarily have sales representatives who visit campuses regularly. If you are interested in talking with one of them, contact the publisher in question and ask to have a sales representative contact you.

Be sure to get your order into your bookstore well enough in advance to ensure that the books are available when the course begins. Be sure as well to order "desk copies" for yourself and for your teaching assistants, if you have them. Many (but not all) publishers will send free copies of course books to instructors if they receive evidence that the book has been adopted; if you can demonstrate a large enrollment, they will usually send multiple copies. They must be ordered separately through the publisher's Web sites. Some publishers have begun charging fees for desk copies and placing other restrictions on them, so do not assume that all your requests will be readily met. But many publishers still distribute free desk copies quite generously, and you should take advantage of such opportunities when you can.

Most institutions and some academic departments maintain DVD, video, and audio collections for the use of faculty and students. If you wish to use any of your school's material, find out what is available and how and when you need to reserve it. But increasingly video and audio materials are available on the Web—sometimes free, sometimes for a modest cost. Purchasing DVDs can be expensive, but many materials can be found inexpensively through online sellers. If there is a DVD series or CD collection that would be particularly useful for a widely taught course, see if your department or library will purchase it. Bowker's Complete Video Directory (three volumes), which is updated every few years, is a useful guide to material on videotape and is available in most libraries. Amazon or the Internet Movie Database might also help you identify available media resources.

Internet-based scholarly networks sponsor electronic discussion groups that often post user suggestions of materials appropriate for a variety of disciplines. They also give you an opportunity to post questions to and solicit suggestions from professional colleagues all over the country (or the world) about your teaching and your research. In addition, many Web sites contain material that can be useful in the classroom.

Photocopied Packets

For decades, many instructors have solved the problem of tailoring assigned reading to their particular needs by making use of packets of photocopied materials, which they then sell to their students. They can include excerpts from books; articles from journals, magazines, or newspapers; primary documents; or material created by the instructor. They become, in effect, the equivalent of a published reader, but one tailored to the precise needs of your course. Some instructors have such packets photocopied by their department or their university, which then makes them available to students for purchase. Others make use of professional photocopying stores, located near most campuses, which make the copies and sell them to students. A photocopied packet can be an excellent way to provide your students with exactly the readings you want to assign them.

But photocopied course packets have serious drawbacks, mostly connected with the copyright laws protecting the original sources. Almost anything published within the last seventy-five years by a commercial or scholarly press is covered by copyright, and it is illegal to sell or distribute copies without receiving permission from the copyright holder and, usually, paying a fee. (Most government documents are not copyrighted and can be copied and distributed at will.) If you are creating an elaborate packet with many different elements, it will be time-consuming and expensive for you to contact all the publishers yourself and arrange the appropriate permissions. But without permissions, you cannot realistically distribute the packet. Commercial photocopiers (some of whom have been the subject of costly lawsuits by publishers over this issue in recent years) will now usually refuse to copy material without the appropriate letters of permission. Your department and university will likely have the same requirements. Many instructors have simply given up on photocopied packets in the face of these seemingly overwhelming difficulties. Commercial photocopiers such as Kinko's sometimes obtain all permissions for you and add the cost of them to the packet before selling it to students. This can save you a great deal of time and aggravation, but it might also add significantly to the cost of the packet and make it unaffordable for your students. Be sure to get an estimate of the final cost before proceeding. Obviously the smaller the packet, or the fewer copyrighted items in it, the lower the cost will be. Increasingly, such materials are migrating onto course Web sites that are restricted to enrolled students.

Articles in many scholarly journals published are now available for free on the Internet through various library databases such as Project Muse, JSTOR, Academic Search Completer, and ERIC, if your university is a participating member. Check with your institution's library to see what databases are available and the terms of their use for faculty and students. Because many databases provide full articles from hundreds of leading journals, you can simply refer students to the Web site. (Be aware that some journals delay recent issues from being added to digital databases for up to five years.) The availability of articles on the Web may significantly reduce the size and cost of your photocopied packet or eliminate the need for one altogether.

Preparing a Syllabus

The syllabus is the central document of your course. It introduces students to your expectations, guides them through assignments, and provides them with a schedule and other important information. If your syllabus is well organized and informative, it can be of enormous value in getting your course properly started and in keeping students on track through the term. The process of preparing a syllabus can be of great value to you, in forcing you to think through the structure and organization of the course, in helping you make decisions about what and how much material you can realistically expect to cover in the short time you have, and in working out how you can best organize that material. Looking at sample syllabi provided by colleagues is helpful, as is looking at those found through various Internet sites, such as History Matters (http://historymatters.gmu.edu/) at George Mason University. See Appendix A for a sample syllabus for a history course.

A good first step in preparing a syllabus is to make, in effect, a calendar of the term. Prepare a list or chart of the weeks, or class days, that your institution's academic calendar makes available to you—and of the specific days on which your class will meet. Take account of holidays and other breaks in the schedule. Then begin scheduling lectures, classes, reading, assignments, and exams accordingly.

As you schedule your assignments, be sensitive to the time pressure students face both in your own course and in others. Don't make a paper due a few days before or after an exam, or the Monday after a homecoming weekend, or the day before Thanksgiving. Don't schedule your heaviest reading assignments for midterm week. Keep in mind that many courses assign papers that are due at the end of the term, and consider whether you can schedule yours earlier to avoid getting caught in the crunch.

The top of the first page of any syllabus should present certain basic information: the name of your institution, the semester and year, the course's full title and number, and (when relevant) the number of credits the course represents. It should also include your own name, your office address, and (depending on your preferences) your telephone number and/or e-mail address. If you know what your office hours will be well enough in advance of the term, you should include those as well.

The syllabus should then provide a brief description of the objectives and procedures of the course. You might include a paragraph or two laying out the central themes, questions, or skills that the course will emphasize. You should certainly explain how the course is structured (how often it will meet and what the format of the meetings will be) and what your expectations are. State clearly what the assignments will be (papers, readings, discussions, labs, exams, etc.) and how much you plan to weight each element in calculating a grade. Students should know whether attendance will be taken and whether class participation is to be included as part of the grade. They should know when papers are due, where they should be handed in, what the procedures are for getting extensions, and what the penalties are for lateness. They should know the dates of exams and the procedures for rescheduling or taking makeups. You may not wish to include all this material on the syllabus itself, particularly if some of these issues are complicated and will take considerable explanation. But the more basic information you place on the syllabus, the less class time you will need to spend explaining rules and procedures.

The syllabus should provide a clear guide to what books students need to buy or borrow at the beginning of the term. As of fall 2010, all courses are required to post a list of assigned books on your school's Web site. You might also provide a simple list of all the reading or other assignments near the beginning of the syllabus, in roughly the order in which you have assigned them—even if you are going to repeat the information later in the course schedule. Students should not have to thumb through a complicated schedule in order to know what books to pick up in the bookstore.

The most important part of the syllabus is usually the weekly or daily schedule of topics and assignments. If you are giving a lecture course, you might list the subjects or titles of your lectures along with the reading assignments that accompany them. If you are teaching a seminar or a discussion course, make clear what material is to be discussed in each class. Even if you have stated due dates for papers and dates for exams at the top of the syllabus, include them again in your schedule. Identify holidays as well.

Some institutions require that every syllabus in every course contain certain information, such as procedures for students with disabilities, a statement of academic honesty, or the final exam schedule. Make sure you are aware of any such mandated information before you complete your syllabus.

You will dramatically reduce the potential for misunderstandings if you are explicit about your goals, expectations, and requirements on the syllabus. Proofread it carefully for errors, match days of the week with corresponding days of the month (few things are more confusing than calendar errors), and review institutional requirements. Then ask yourself about the tone of your syllabus. If you were a student reading this syllabus for the first time, what impression would you have of the course and of the teacher? The syllabus should give an accurate impression of both you and the course it describes.

Finally, be aware of the limits of your preparation. Despite the most careful planning and preparation, no course will follow your expectations exactly. As important as it is to prepare carefully in advance, it is also important, from the first day of class, to be attentive to your students' reactions and performances and to be flexible enough to make changes when you think they may be helpful to your class or when things are going wrong.

The First Few Weeks

The first few weeks of the term may well be the most difficult for you, particularly if you are a new teacher. But they are also the weeks in which the character of a course and the reputation of the instructor are established. If your students are not drawn into the material you wish them to learn at the beginning, it could be more difficult to improve things as you move along.

Preparing for the First Class

The first day of class is particularly important, especially if you are new to the classroom. It is also the day when you will likely be the most nervous. It might help to remember that your students may be as nervous as you are. (Just as students often have anxiety dreams about walking unprepared into an exam, many teachers have similar dreams before a term begins about walking unprepared into a lecture or class.)

In preparing for your first class, you should, of course, prepare intellectually; you need to know the material you will be asking your students to learn. Equally important, especially if you are a new teacher, is deciding on a style and tone that will be effective in the classroom. The first rule of thumb is to choose a classroom style that is comfortable for you. Do not try to make your classroom persona wholly different from your normal self. Students will usually recognize an artificial posture sooner or later, and you will probably be unable to sustain an unnatural teaching style for very long in any case. But that does not mean that you should behave in the classroom exactly as you would behave in other places. Your instincts may tell you to be casual and informal; but you will also need to convey that you take them and the project you are beginning with them seriously, and that they should do the same. If you begin a class with at least a small amount of formality, it is relatively easy to move from there to a friendlier and more casual tone later. It is much more difficult to reverse the process.

Think carefully about how you wish to present yourself in the classroom. What you wear, how you address your students (first names, last names), how you ask them to address you, whether you stand or sit or pace—all of these things help establish your style and identity in the students' minds. Consider what kind of relationship you wish to establish with your students, and behave in ways that are consistent with it. Decide in advance how you wish to communicate with your students outside the classroom. Do you wish to give students your home phone number? This is usually not a good idea, especially for teachers whose families need their attention. Do you want to encourage students to communicate with you by e-mail? This may raise expectations of responsiveness and reduce the likelihood that students will come to see you during office hours. Establish the ground rules of your relationship with them early to avoid misunderstandings later.

The physical arrangement of your classroom can make a difference too. In many cases, you may have no control over how a classroom is arranged. But if you do, think about the configuration with which you will feel most comfortable. If you are teaching in a room with movable desks or chairs, decide whether you want students to sit in a circle, as if around a seminar table, to facilitate discussion, or in rows facing forward, to facilitate lectures and presentations. Visit the room in advance and think about what possibilities, and problems, it presents.

How do you want to arrive in class? Arriving early and talking with students as they walk in may help you, and them, to relax. Arriving at just the moment the class is scheduled to begin may help you avoid possible awkwardness in switching from casual conversation to the more structured dynamics of the actual class. Arriving late is not an acceptable option.

Deciding What to Teach on the First Day of Class

The best way to know how to start any class is to give students a clear sense of what you expect them to achieve in your course. Make clear what your requirements will be. Establish whatever rules you think are appropriate. But also use your first class to give students at least a preliminary taste of the substance of your course. Some teachers simply start at the beginning, and make few concessions to the fact that students are there for the first time. They say, in effect, we are here to do something important, and we are going to start doing it without delay. Other teachers use the first class to offer an engaging sample of what they want their students to learn. They might assign an exercise that will give students the experience of mastering a technique or a small body of knowledge right away. They might present a lecture that tells a particularly vivid or captivating story that will capture students' interest early in the course. They might distribute a document or problem set and invite students to respond to it, giving them a hands-on experience of interpretation or analysis or methodology from the outset. Whatever you do, pick something you care about and can teach with energy.

The first class, naturally, is also the time to distribute your syllabus and to explain procedural matters. If you have prepared your syllabus well, you should not have to spend too much time discussing the mechanics of the course. But be sure to devote at least some time to establishing procedures and answering students' questions. If you expect the procedural discussion to be brief, you might wish to get it out of the way at the very beginning of class. If you expect it to be long and complicated, you might save it for the last part of the class and use your first minutes with your students to deal with something more interesting and challenging.

In some institutions students are encouraged to "shop" for courses before selecting them. Because many students may be deciding whether or not they wish to take your course, give them an experience on the first day that will show them what you think is best about it—but also one that will give them a sense of what is expected of them. Students who are unwilling to participate in a class discussion, for example, should learn immediately that your class is not appropriate for them if you value participation. Some students may miss your first day's class because they are observing other teachers, and some students who come the first day may not return. So don't organize your course so rigidly that a change in enrollment will derail your plans.

One of the most important things you can do on the first day of a class in which discussion and participation are at the heart of the effort is to find a way to get everyone to say at least something. Try to elicit thoughts from students who seem reluctant to talk. Establish immediately that this is a shared enterprise, that students are expected to be active participants in your joint project, not passive observers.

Making Introductions

In a very large class, it may be unrealistic to ask students to introduce themselves to each other and to you. Even in a smaller class, the chaos of the first day—especially in a school where students may not yet be committed to the course—can be a difficult time for introductions. But sooner or later you should devote some time to having the students introduce themselves. Introductions can take many forms. The simplest is just to ask students to tell the class who they are. But if fifteen or twenty students simply state their names one after the other, neither you nor they are likely to learn or remember very much from the experience. More productive is encouraging students to say something of substance about themselves—where they are from, what interests or activities they are involved in outside of class, or what their majors or their academic interests are. Some instructors ask students to think of one interesting fact about themselves and present it to the class. Others ask students to introduce not themselves, but the person sitting next to them; each student "interviews" the other and then presents the results.

Of course, you should introduce yourself as well. But since you are older and more experienced, you may have a great deal more to tell about yourself than they do. Keep your own introduction relatively short so as not to create an impossible standard for your students when they present theirs, but say enough to give them a sense of what an appropriate introduction should be. You can also introduce yourself after the students are done.

Establishing the Dynamics of a Classroom

Many good teachers try to establish from the beginning that they expect their students to be active participants in the classroom—that the purpose of the course is not teaching, but learning. That usually means requiring students to take some responsibility for the conduct of the course and to take some risks in the process of learning. Since many students may find such expectations new and unusual, you may need to reassure them. If you are teaching a large course in which you have limited personal contact with your students, the task of motivating them comes from how you present yourself to them and what you ask them to do on their own. But in smaller courses, where it is possible to know your students, there are many more opportunities—and sometimes many more problems.

In defining the dynamics of your class, first think carefully about how close you wish to become to your students. If you are too much a "friend," especially if you are young, you may diminish your effectiveness. You might develop inappropriate relationships with your students. An accusation of sexual harassment or other inappropriate behavior can destroy a professional career irrevocably—not to mention the damage an inappropriate relationship can do to a student. Most instructors would not consider initiating or entering such a relationship, but even they should be careful to do nothing that might be misunderstood.

On the other hand, avoiding an inappropriate relationship does not mean having no relationship with students. It is perfectly appropriate, often even desirable, to have friendly relationships with students, to meet with them outside of class, even to have social interaction with them. You might take students for lunch or for coffee—preferably in groups, and preferably in settings that are appropriate for that purpose. You might invite them to your home for dinner—again, especially if you are single, usually in groups, not individually. It is probably not a good idea for an instructor, even a graduate instructor, to attend undergraduate parties at which his or her students may be present, or to take students out drinking.

Whatever you decide, you should, if possible, know who your students are. Some teachers use a roster with photos before a class meets to learn and memorize names, but most teachers have no such option. Careful introductions at the beginning can help. So can asking students to state their names briefly at the beginning of subsequent classes to allow them to remind you and each other of who they are. (Make sure to ask all students, even those you know, to introduce—or reintroduce—themselves to avoid revealing which names you have not learned.) You might also ask them to identify themselves when making a comment in class during the first few meetings, and request that they sit in the same seats each week until you learn their names. If you are not good at remembering names, be open about it and make clear that you will be making a real effort to overcome the problem. Or ask students to place their names on small signs in front of them, and explain that this is to help you learn their names and also to help them get to know one another. Nothing is more dispiriting to students in a small class than a sense that the instructor does not know who they are. Worst of all is when a teacher learns some names and not others; those whose names the teacher does not learn can easily come to feel anonymous and marginal.

Find out what you can about your students—their majors, their interests, their backgrounds. Introductions at the beginning of the term are one way to do this. You might also ask students to fill out note cards giving you their names, contact information, and some pertinent facts about themselves, so that you will have a record to which you can refer. If you know something about your students, you can target your questions more effectively and often give reticent students a chance to participate more comfortably.

Help your students to know each other. The more students get to know one another, the more comfortable they will feel interacting with one another—both in and out of class. Here again, introductions—the more informative the better—can help. It also helps to distribute a list of everyone in the class early in the term, with names, addresses, phone numbers, e-mail addresses, and so forth (although you should be sure to ask students for permission before you distribute any information about them to others). Getting students involved early in the term in projects or assignments that require collaboration is another good way to help them feel comfortable with and connected to one another.

Perhaps most important, treat your students with respect. Do not belittle them. Do not embarrass them in front of their peers. Do not confuse browbeating and intimidating with motivating. There was a time when it was common in higher education for larger-than-life teachers to tyrannize students and intimidate them into working harder. But in today's academic culture, such tactics will usually seem bizarre and alienating.

Dealing with Passive, Voluble, or Disruptive Students

Teachers often find that there are problem students in the class. It is very important, therefore, to establish your ground rules for dealing with students who are passive, excessively voluble, or openly disruptive.

Most classes include some students who participate actively and others who remain passive. In dealing with passive students, it is important first to try to understand why they are silent. In some cases, you may find otherwise voluble students remaining quiet because they have taken some dislike to the class or to you. If you sense that is the case, you might try to have a conversation with the students in question outside of class to try to find out what the problem is. Unchecked, alienation of that sort can infect others. More often, however, passive students are quiet because they are intimidated by you or the class, or have convinced themselves—or been convinced by others—that they have nothing of interest to offer.

There may be some students who are so shy or so insecure that no amount of prompting will draw them effectively into the dynamic of the classroom. But you should nevertheless make a serious effort to engage all your students, and you should begin those efforts at the start of the term so that your expectations are clear and students can immediately begin to feel comfortable speaking in the group. The simplest and most obvious way is to encourage quiet students to speak is to call on them rather than waiting for them to volunteer. You might arrange to meet with such students individually outside class, explain the importance of participation, and try to prepare them for the next discussion. You might share with the student in advance a question that you plan to raise in the next class. Or you might ask students to work together in small groups—either before or during part of a class—to prepare a presentation or an argument. Some students who seem unusually reticent in the structured setting of a class discussion are much more relaxed in small, less formal groups.

Excessively talkative students, no matter how gifted, can present an equally serious problem. If a student dominates a class so thoroughly that other students are unable to participate adequately, you need to act. One way to do so is to talk with garrulous students outside class: assure them that you value their comments, but make clear to them that they must restrain themselves and make space for other students to participate. In the classroom itself, you can prevent a single student from dominating the class by taking charge of the discussion so that you are the one who chooses who is to speak, as opposed to allowing the conversation to flow spontaneously. It is always difficult to interrupt or cut off students, and teachers are usually (and appropriately) reluctant to embarrass them by doing so. But in some cases, an interruption is essential to the dynamic of the class as a whole.

Sometimes students intentionally or inadvertently become disruptive. It can be a relatively passive disruption—for example, students who read, text, check e-mail, or work on other material while you are teaching. It is perfectly appropriate to ask such students to stop—or even to ask them not to open computers at all in the classroom. It is also sometimes helpful, if you wish to avoid a direct confrontation, to wait until the beginning of the next class and simply announce to everyone that it is not acceptable for students to read or do other work while you are teaching. You may also encounter active disruption. Students may get in the habit of coming late or leaving early; make clear to them—and to everyone—that you expect them to come and go on schedule. (Some students have legitimate reasons to come late or leave early on certain days, in which case you should insist that they notify you in advance; and you might consider explaining to the rest of the class why one student is violating the policy to make clear that they should not do the same.)

Some students may say antagonistic or explosive things to see how you will react. If the comment, whatever its intent, is worthy of a serious response, then take it seriously—and ask other students to respond to it. Some kinds of comments are simply offensive, and intolerable in class. They must be challenged, even rebuked. State clearly, if such problems arise, that you will not tolerate certain kinds of remarks in class (for example, comments disparaging a person's race, gender, appearance, or sexual orientation), and you should react even more forcefully if they are directed at other members of the class.

Establishing the Dynamics of Office Hours

Some instructors may have many opportunities to meet with students outside of class. For most, however, the usual occasion other than class time for meeting students is office hours. Just as it is important to establish the dynamic of your classroom early, you should also establish the character of your office hours from the start.

The most important thing for you to do during your office hours is to be there. It may frustrate and anger your students if they come to your office at the appointed time and not find you. During office hours, leave your door open unless you are already in a conversation with a student and feel that privacy is important. Some students may interpret a closed door as a signal that you are busy or unavailable, so you should make sure that students who are waiting to talk with you understand that a closed door means that you are busy with another student.

Schedule your office hours at times likely to be convenient for your students. Early Monday morning and late Friday afternoon are bad times. Immediately before or after class is often a good time. If there are students who are consistently unable to make your office hours because of other commitments, try to find other times to talk with them. Encourage students who have trouble matching their schedules with yours to use e-mail, which can, in effect, extend your office hours and make them accessible to busy students. It surely makes it more difficult for students to claim that you are not available.

If you have your own office, by all means use it. But if necessary establish an appropriate place—a professor's vacant office, an empty classroom, a place in the library where talking is permitted, if necessary a table in a coffee shop or cafeteria (ideally a quiet one)—where you can conduct meetings regularly. Avoid using your home, or any other non-public place. Students may feel uncomfortable and even misinterpret your motives.

Getting students to visit you during office hours requires some effort on your part. That begins with active encouragement in class—making clear that you are not only available but eager to see students. It can also help to establish requirements. If the course is small enough, you might require each student to schedule a meeting with you. (Requiring such meetings has the additional advantage of giving you a structured opportunity to talk with students who are having, or causing, problems without singling them out.) After students have come to see you once, even if involuntarily, the prospect of coming again will seem less intimidating. In larger classes, in particular, you might consider group sessions, in which you invite several students to come to your office together for an appointment.

When a student arrives in your office, put down any other work you are doing immediately. Don't answer the phone while the student is there, or if you must, keep your conversation brief. Most important, try to determine why the student has come to you. Often, this will be obvious. Students will have questions about assignments, will want extensions on papers, or will have specific questions about material you've covered in class. Sometimes, however, students will come to office hours simply to meet you but will not be certain what to do once they are there. You can help by asking them to tell you something about themselves and otherwise suggesting that you are pleased to see them and interested in talking with them. At other times, students will have problems—intellectual or personal—that they want to discuss with you but are afraid to bring up. Again, it is important for you to show an interest in them and not express impatience when they are not immediately clear about what they want.

Although you should never dismiss a legitimate concern or question from a student, you should not agree to inappropriate requests either. Students who have missed many classes and assignments and want you to "fill them in" are not making reasonable requests. Tell them what they can do to catch up, but stress that it is their responsibility, not yours.

Do not attempt to take on burdens beyond your expertise or experience. Listen respectfully and sympathetically to personal problems and help if you think you can. But many issues are outside your area of expertise. Be familiar with the support services of your institution so that you can, if necessary, refer a student to a trained professional. Remember that you can sometimes do more harm than good if you try to help a student with an emotional or mental health issue that you do not fully understand. If you sense that a student is in truly serious difficulty, notify the appropriate dean or other official immediately to ensure that someone monitors the situation.

Sometimes individual students may try to monopolize your time—because they like you, because they think spending time with you will benefit them in some way, or because they are naturally garrulous. It is important to find a gracious way of limiting the time one student can spend with you, especially when there are other students waiting or you have appointments pending. Keeping the door open during office hours so that your visitors can see whether other students are waiting can help here. Doing so may discourage a single student from staying too long. But if necessary, it is perfectly appropriate, after a reasonable period, to tell a student that you must now speak with the next person in line. Or you can begin each session with a statement that you cannot speak indefinitely because other students are waiting or are expected.

In teaching, nothing is certain. But if you organize a course carefully, begin a class effectively, and prepare your students fully for what you expect of them; if you establish a cordial, even lively atmosphere in your classroom; if you convince your students that you are interested in them and their work—then your chances of success will greatly improve.

Active and Collaborative Learning

The ability to involve students as active participants in their own learning is central to effective teaching. Discussions of various kinds are the most common form of teaching at almost all levels, and for many students and teachers the most challenging and rewarding. A successful discussion is an exciting, even a memorable, experience for everyone involved, and one of the great joys of teaching. Other types of collaborative learning, such as simulations, role-playing, and debates, if planned well, allow students to not only engage with the subject but to be creative as well.

Leading or facilitating a discussion, debate, or simulation can be one of the most difficult and unpredictable of all teaching experiences. Most teachers know the feeling of coming to the end of a class excited and eager for more. But virtually all teachers also know the feeling of trying to create a good discussion or debate and failing. Some things may be partially or wholly outside your control. Many teachers have had the experience of doing the same things with the same material in two different classrooms and having entirely different results. Sometimes activities fail—or at least fail to sparkle—no matter what you do. But there are techniques by which you can make failure less likely.

Varieties of Classroom Discussion

Classroom discussions take many different forms, from large lecture courses in which instructors elicit student participation (see chapter 4) to very small seminars or even tutorials in which the discussion becomes something close to a personal conversation.

Despite the differences among various forms of discussion, some things are common to almost all of them. They are not simply occasions for interesting conversations or for students to have opportunities to talk. They are also occasions for students—to receive information, to consider arguments, to develop skills, or to test ideas. However student centered the discussion may be, the instructor must be ready to intervene to ensure that it remains productive.

One common method of leading a discussion is for the instructor to orchestrate the conversation through Socratic methods: asking questions, responding to the answers, and asking more questions, trying to lead the class in the direction the teacher has previously decided it should go. Perhaps the most famous example of the Socratic discussion in modern education is the traditional law school classroom dialogue between students and professor, which—at least as presented in film and on television—is often a tense, even confrontational fencing match. In other settings, however, such discussions are usually more informal and less confrontational. A teacher can combine traditional "instruction" with student participation. Such discussions often take place in traditional classrooms, with the instructors in the front of the room and the students facing the teachers from desks or tables arranged in rows or semicircles; but they can, of course, take place in any setting.

A very different kind of discussion, generally associated with the concept of the seminar, is one in which the teacher tries to serve mainly as a mediator and guide to a conversation among the students themselves. A seminar instructor usually asks questions of the students, at least at the beginning of class, but less to elicit particular answers and lead the class along a rigidly predetermined path than to stimulate conversation and debate among the students. These discussions often occur around a seminar table, with the instructor usually seated either at the head of the table, if it is rectangular, or randomly among the students, if the table is round or square. If there is no table, and the chairs or desks in the classroom are movable, a teacher can prepare for a seminar discussion by having students arrange their seats in a circle. It is difficult to run a seminar in a conventional classroom with fixed desks all facing forward, but it is not impossible—and there may be times when that is the only space available.

A Socratic discussion can take place in a class of almost any size, although the larger the class, the more inhibited students are likely to be about speaking up. (The famous law school Socratic dialogues often involve hundreds of students, but in those classes the professor usually selects people to question at random from a class list; that technique is much more difficult in undergraduate courses, with their more heterogeneous populations.) A seminar discussion is difficult to sustain in a group of more than twenty students, and works best with a group of eight to fifteen.

Preparing for a Discussion

Preparation is at least as critical to a successful discussion as it is to a successful lecture. Indeed, some instructors use lecture-like outlines in preparing for a class discussion (although those who do so often have great difficulty steering their class along the route they have prepared). Most teachers prepare in a less rigidly structured way. But however you prepare, try to follow certain basic steps in getting ready for your class.

First, be familiar with the material your students are gathering to discuss. Second, as in any class, have goals for your discussion: issues you want your students to consider, questions you want them to answer, or problems you want them to encounter. You may, and probably should, be reasonably flexible about how they reach the goals you have set and whether they reach all of them, but you should be ready to ensure that they reach some of them. If, as is often the case, the points you wish the discussion to address build on one another, try to have a rough idea of the sequence you want the class to follow—the question with which you want them to begin, and the order in which you want them to move through the material. You may find that you do not need to follow the plan you have made. But it is always a good idea to have a plan of your own, in case you find you need it.

Students need to prepare for discussions just as much as the instructor, and in a course that depends on participation you need to make clear at the start that everyone should be ready and willing to play an active role in class. Usually, such preparation will mean doing assigned reading or other exercises; and thus much of the task of ensuring adequate preparation rests on encouraging students to complete these assignments before they come to class. Giving your students some insight into the assignments in advance—either by talking about them in an earlier class or distributing questions and guidelines for readings or exercises before the discussion—can help lead them into material that some might otherwise find obscure. But if encouragement and exhortation are not enough, you can try some slightly more coercive tactics: assigning a short paper on the topic ahead of time that will require them to think about the material you will be discussing, or giving a brief in-class writing assignment on the reading at the start of the class period.

A different way of motivating students to prepare for class is to make a regular habit of calling on all members of the group, even letting students know that you intend to grade them in some way on their participation. Some instructors create a "discussion note card" for each student and then shuffle them to determine whom they will question. The instructor can then mark on the note card the date the student was randomly selected and how well he or she responded. But the best way to motivate students is to help them become excited about the subject, the class, the assignments, and even about you.

Starting a Discussion

Beginning a discussion is often difficult, particularly early in the term, when the students do not yet know one another, or you, very well. Simply asking your class what they thought of the assignment for the week can lead to a painful silence; that may be too big a question for most students to know how to answer right away. It is better to give them something more specific to consider, such as a brief document or problem set, and then ask for responses. You might write on the blackboard a series of questions or ideas from an earlier class or assignment. You might ask the students to write a thesis statement or topic sentence on a subject you wish to discuss and then have one or two students read their efforts aloud. Or you might simply begin with a deliberately provocative question that you feel certain will inspire disagreement.

It is useful to start most discussions with questions that can lead in multiple directions—questions that do not have a single, simple answer. Good discussions thrive on disagreement, and a question or set of questions that launches a debate will be more effective than straightforward, linear questions that lead in only one direction. Short questions with long answers are usually much better than the reverse.

Many instructors assign students to lead, or at least launch, the discussion each week, which has the advantage of giving them an experience of thinking through the subject and trying to present ideas in class. But students may be less successful than you would be in generating discussion among their peers, so be prepared to step in if their efforts to stimulate participation flag. Students will often be more successful in launching a discussion if you have started the class yourself once or twice and have given them an example of the kinds of questions and classroom styles that work. They are also likely to be more successful if they are working in teams and are thus forced to have conversations about the material with one another before they try leading a conversation in the classroom. The team or group approach often works well for initiating a discussion in class; students have the chance to discuss a topic among a small group of their peers before the entire class.

Sustaining a Discussion

Once the discussion has begun, even if it is proceeding smoothly on its own, students will be watching for your reactions to what they say. You may be entirely silent, but your facial expressions and body language can have a major impact on what students think about their own comments, or those of others. Positive reinforcement—smiling, nodding, complimenting—can be helpful in encouraging a discussion, although only if your encouragement is spread fairly widely around the class. Avoid discouraging conversation with negative expressions or gestures, even inadvertent ones. In any case, remember that you will never be just another participant in a discussion. Your behavior—both spoken and physical—will always have a significant influence on how your class behaves and perceives itself.

Even a successful, self-sustaining conversation will require your intervention from time to time—to move the discussion in the directions you think it should go, or to rescue it from students who are taking it off track. Be constantly alert to signs that the discussion is bogging down, becoming repetitive, or moving away from the issues you think are important. When it does, you need to step in and try to redirect it.

One of the most difficult questions facing any discussion leader is how to deal with students who are making mistakes or missing the point. Do not let misinformation or misdirection go unanswered, but do not discourage or embarrass the students who are responsible for the problems. If possible, find something positive to say about even the most wrongheaded remark—before refuting or correcting a student's comment. If a student has said something intelligent or interesting, even if incorrect, you might respond with a comment such as "That's a great wrong answer," which will encourage further discussion of the response. Sometimes, of course, students will argue with and correct each other in a discussion, and in that case the best thing for you to do is stay out of the way. But when a comment or question is directed at you, always make sure that you respond somehow—with praise, with criticism, with another question aimed at the group. And when significant errors go uncorrected by other students, be sure to correct them—gently.

Leading a discussion often requires considerable patience. When you ask a question or raise an issue, give your students some time to think before calling on anyone to speak. Avoid calling on the first raised hand, especially if it goes up very quickly, which suggests that the student in question has not thought much about what he or she is going to say. Make sure students know that in the first moments of class a thoughtful silence is perfectly appropriate. If no one responds to a question after a few moments, ask yourself if you have framed it badly and need to refocus it. Keep rephrasing it, and adding more information, until students know enough to respond to it.

Even seemingly simple decisions can have a big impact on a discussion. For example, should you stand or sit? In a small seminar, it makes sense to sit at the table (or in a circle of chairs) with the students, to make it clear that you are all part of a conversation together—and to make your own temporary withdrawal from a lively, self-sustaining discussion easier. But with a larger or a more reticent group, especially one in which you are using Socratic methods, it often makes sense to stand and to move strategically around the room as a way of creating a sense of energy and engagement. Your physical presence can have a significant effect on a discussion. For example, if you are trying to encourage students to challenge one another, consider standing behind a student being challenged to avoid having the challenger feel torn between addressing remarks to you and addressing them to a peer.

How you use the blackboard can also affect the character of a discussion. You can use the board to chart the progress of a discussion, to draw attention to particularly important questions, to pose choices, to write passages of text to be analyzed or problems to be solved. (If you do use the blackboard, be sure that your writing is legible and is large enough to be read by the students seated farthest from it.) You can also ask students themselves to use the board to work out ideas or problems they are trying to resolve.

Some discussions, particularly in larger classes, will always be guided by the instructor. But in many cases, particularly in smaller classes, there is a different goal. A seminar instructor will usually strive to get a discussion to a place where the students, not the teacher, are in control—where there is enough commitment to the conversation, and enough interest in the questions it raises, that it can continue without you. Getting to that point can be very difficult and requires patience, flexibility, and sometimes considerable prodding. But when a discussion takes on a life of its own, stand back—at least for a while—and let it build, intervening gently only when you feel it necessary to steer the conversation back to the issues you want students to address.

Reviving a Lagging Discussion

Even the best planned and directed discussion can fail to take off. A stalled discussion is always uncomfortable for both students and teacher, and there are times when nothing you do will rekindle it effectively. But there are also techniques for jump-starting a flagging discussion that will work more often than not.

One way to help ensure that your discussions do not flag irretrievably is to establish from the start that students should come to every class prepared to report on something: a document of their choosing, related to the topic for the week, which they are to bring with them to class; a reading journal they are asked to keep; or a question they are asked to prepare. If all your students understand that they are liable to be called on without warning to give a short oral response, they are likely to be better prepared for class than if they feel confident that they can sit silently without fear of reproach. And if the discussion does flag, you have an immediate recourse—ask one of your students to give a quick report.

Playing the devil's advocate—taking an outrageous position on an issue to try to provoke rejoinders—can be effective in igniting a discussion, although it runs the risk of offending or confusing students. Always signal your class when taking this approach. Using analogies to current events or to contemporary popular culture can sometimes help; almost everyone will have something to say about current political controversy or a currently popular film or television show. But here, too, you have to be careful; you don't want a discussion of *Moby Dick* to turn into a discussion of *American Idol*. Another approach to a faltering discussion is to ask students to read something aloud, such as a passage from the text assigned for the week or a document you (or they) have brought to class. You can then focus discussion on that for a while and hope students will pick up the thread from there. Counterfactual questions—would America have become bogged down in Vietnam if John Kennedy had lived; how would we evaluate F. Scott Fitzgerald if he had not written *The Great Gatsby;* how would the U.S. government be different if there were no Senate—can often open up new avenues of discussion. Even a simple, objective question—a question with a single, correct answer—might give students a way back into a discussion that has lost its way. All such approaches are, in effect, devices, whose principal value is in stirring students to speak. Try not to stick with any of them for too long.

Both a successful and a flagging discussion will often profit from many different kinds of questions, used strategically at different times depending on the circumstances. Linear questions, which can discourage discussion at the beginning of class, may help revive it later. Open-ended questions, with many possible answers, can get a discussion going; but they can also increase the tension in a room where a discussion has gone awry. It is important to learn how to use the right kinds of questions in the right places. Being a successful discussion leader may not come naturally or quickly; but if you make an effort to analyze your own performance and test new techniques, you will almost certainly get better over time.

Bringing a Discussion to an End

The concluding moments of any class discussion are very important. You don't want a discussion simply to run out of steam or out of time. You want, rather, to lead the discussion to some kind of satisfactory conclusion that will leave students with a sense of what they have, or should have, learned. You can conclude with remarks of your own, summarizing or clarifying important points. You can ask your students to offer a summary of the arguments themselves. You can signal what you will be considering at the next meeting or what unanswered questions you will want the class to return to later. But whatever you do, and however briefly you do it, be sure that there is a clear conclusion. Do not let the discussion simply fizzle out or stop abruptly at the end of the period.

But do end class on time. Students have other courses and obligations, and they are rightly annoyed when an instructor keeps them late.

Helping Students Teach Themselves through Collaborative Learning

The classroom discussion, in all its many varieties, is the most common form of teaching and learning in relatively small groups. But many instructors use discussions as a means to involve their students in group work or use other techniques that delegate more responsibility to the student. Educational theorists make a distinction between teaching and learning, and some argue that traditional classroom methods do not do enough to make students active participants in their own learning process. Collaborative teaching and other techniques can give students a more direct role in their own education. Delegating work and authority to students does not, however, mean that your role is any less important. On the contrary, student-centered learning is highly dependent on the instructor's guidance and participation.

Instructors can engage students in collective learning processes through a variety of methods. One of the simplest—and a very good way to ensure that even relatively quiet students have the experience of participating in discussions—is simply to divide your class into small groups, each of which will have its own discussion about some aspect of the day's material. After a certain period of time, you can bring the class back together and ask each group to report on the results of its discussion. You can ask several groups to discuss the same question and then see what different perspectives result. Or you can ask each group to evaluate a different portion of an assignment or problem, and then try to put the different reports together at the end. You can start with one set of groups and then use a jig-saw to rescramble them to bring the perspectives of different groups into contact with one another.

While students are meeting in smaller groups, you might choose to leave the room for a while to make clear to them that they are now in charge of the learning process. You might just stand or sit to the side until the time comes for the group discussions to come to a close. You might move from group to group, listening and answering questions if any are asked, but not usually intervening otherwise and certainly not directing the discussion. (Some teachers take down phrases heard in each group and write them on the blackboard as a way to help bring the discussions together once the group reports are completed.) If you do join a group, you should sit down with the students. Standing above them while they are sitting can intimidate them and erode their sense of having control over their work.

Group activities may take different formats. You can assign students to work together on some aspect of an assignment and prepare a report or PowerPoint presentation to deliver to the class. You can send students out together to research a question and ask them to develop materials that they can distribute or display to others. You can stage debates, mock trials, and other simulations. You can make several students responsible for launching a discussion or summarizing it at the end. You can involve students in a collective project (producing a collaborative report on an issue, creating a multiauthored journal, or publishing material on the Internet or on a class site within Blackboard or a similar program), in which everyone has responsibilities to everyone else. With these and many other techniques, you can help students feel both a sense of responsibility to the class and a sense of control over their own learning.

Be sure to give students guidance in advance, so that they will understand what they are going to do and what is expected of them. Try as well to encourage students to negotiate responsibilities among themselves when they are working on collaborative projects, and perhaps to choose a group leader or a secretary to help them organize or record their work. If the class is dividing up into groups and you know the students well enough to sense who might work well together, you may wish to make the assignments yourself. If you do not know the students well enough to feel confident in your judgment, you should probably organize the groups more or less randomly. When you allow students to form their own groups, you run the risk of putting groups of friends together, of excluding some students, or of creating racial, gender, or intellectual divisions or imbalances.

Organizing students into self-directed groups does not guarantee that all students will participate in the group's work. Some students may be as passive in a small-group effort as they are in the class as a whole; some might be even more passive, assuming that in your absence nothing important is at stake. To guard against this problem, you might insist that each member of a group participate in the group's report to the class. You might assign each student a paper based on the group work. You might design a grading system in which everyone's grade in the group is affected by the quality of everyone else's answers. (This approach also ensures that stronger students develop their own teaching skills, since they will have a stake in ensuring that everyone in their group learns and contributes something.)

Simulation Exercises

Simulation is an especially elaborate and structured form of group activity. In a simulation, students assume the roles of actors in the material they are studying: historical figures, policy makers, literary characters or critics, and so forth. They drop their accustomed roles as detached observers of the issues they are studying and become, for a time, active participants in the events or ideas they are being asked to understand. In a small way, simulations can play something of the role in the humanities and social sciences that laboratories play in the natural sciences.

If you are planning a simulation, assign students their roles in advance. Consider asking students to "play against type." For example, require a conservative student to take the part of a radical. Consider too whether a particular student has a particular interest in a particular character or issue. Finally, bear in mind individual ability, but also bear in mind the need to promote creativity, responsibility, and hilarity—simulations often enable classes to bond around a shared laugh.

Be careful not to present the students with an impossible task. Always make sure that sufficient material exists to allow them to understand or infer what their characters might think or argue. It is also a good idea to check in advance on availability—are the resources readily available in your library, through interlibrary loan, on the Internet, or in a form that you can provide?

Before the activity begins, you might have the students write papers based on their characters or roles. When you return them, ideally before the simulation starts, you can include suggestions for additional reading and preparation. Or, if time permits, hold individual conferences with students to verify that they understand their roles and responsibilities. By the time the simulation starts, students should have spent considerable time preparing for it. After the simulation concludes, you might have all students write a paper based on the exercise. These papers will help them make sense of the usually unfamiliar experience they have just had. The student reflections will also help you get a sense of how successful the simulation was.

Popular simulations include trials of presidents who were never impeached, debates over constitutional amendments that were never proposed, and discussions by literary characters of their motives or fiction writers of their work (even if they lived in different eras). Simulations can also attempt to recreate real events, but with no expectation that the activity will replicate reality. A simulated Constitutional Convention might well lead to a Congress without a Senate, or a president limited to a single term. (See Appendix B for an example of a trial of Karl Marx used in a world history course.)

Commercially packaged simulations, usually in the form of games, do exist, but you will probably enjoy more success if you design the simulation on your own, or in collaboration with your students. Focus on important issues. Simulations are time-consuming, so avoid issues or topics you consider unimportant. Try to involve all students at all times in the simulation—remember that the primary goal is active learning. Making some students witnesses and others attorneys while most are jurors ensures that many will become little more than passive observers. If possible, have students instead assume multiple roles, such as witness and juror.

Try not to intervene during a simulation, although you may want to create small windows from time to time where you can offer comments and corrections (if necessary). Allow students to make mistakes, and be reasonably tolerant of an exercise that is not going as planned. But if a simulation (or any other independent group activity) goes badly awry, or breaks down altogether—either because of inadequate preparation by you or the students, or because of some unforeseen difficulty—do not hesitate to restart the simulation or end it prematurely. Sometimes it is necessary to admit defeat or failure, no matter how painful.

Debates and Panel Discussions

Classroom debates or panel discussions may be more familiar to you and to your students than simulations. They are also easier to organize. But many of the same techniques are useful here as well. As with a simulation, the critical factor is the choice of topic. Choose something students will find important or exciting. Give students a chance to prepare, either individually or collectively in teams. Consider providing resource material for each team or at least a bibliography of available resources. Do not create debates in which large numbers of students are passive observers for long periods. During the debate itself, give nonparticipating students chances to ask questions of the participants. Leave time at the end for the class as a whole to assess the results, perhaps by choosing the team with the more effective arguments. (See Appendix B for an example of a debate used in a U.S. history course.)

Whatever topic you pick, consider having the students produce some sort of short paper before the activity and a second short paper after it. Without closure students will listen politely to the other presentations but will never have a reason to take close notes or to rethink the arguments made in class.

Other Forms of Collaborative Learning

The examples presented here are only a few of the many ways in which you can move beyond the lecture or traditional discussion and encourage students to play a more active role in learning. Some of the most important collaborative learning experiences can occur outside the classroom: students can engage in joint research projects, produce short films or Web sites together, or create a class journal. The Internet can facilitate important new forms of learning as well by making it possible for students to publish the results of their work. (Chapter 10 offers suggestions on how to use the Internet and other electronic tools.) You or your students may discover other forms of self-generated or collaborative learning as you move through the term. In fact, one of the best ways to encourage such learning is to include students in the process of conceiving and planning it.

Handing responsibility for learning over to the students can yield enormous rewards of excitement, engagement, and innovation. But be careful to adjust your techniques and your expectations to your own circumstances. And be prepared to intervene and provide direction to the class when circumstances require it.

4

The Art and Craft of Lecturing

Delivering lectures is one of the oldest forms of teaching at the college and university level and is still, perhaps, the most common. It has many critics. Some educational theorists argue that lectures are passive experiences for students and undermine their efforts to become actively engaged in the learning process. Others argue that lectures are obsolete, that they simply present in spoken form material that can be more effectively presented in written (including electronic) form and distributed to students.

But lecturing has survived generations of criticism and is likely to survive many more. One reason is simple economics. Large colleges and universities often do not have the resources to permit all teaching to be conducted in intimate classes where discussion and active student participation are the norm. But there are other, and better, justifications for lecturing as a valuable form of teaching as well. A series of lectures is a form of pedagogy that has no counterpart elsewhere. It represents a teacher's effort to understand a large body of knowledge, synthesize it, and present it to students in a way that he or she believes makes sense. It is, at its best, a thematic exercise, in which the lecturer makes conscious and deliberate choices about what kinds of material to discuss and what meaning to assign to it. And it is an extended exercise. A typical lecture course requires an instructor to present twenty to thirty lectures in a term, which in turn produces a steady accumulation of information and, ideally, a clearly charted path through the material—from a starting point to a conclusion. Most of all, perhaps, lectures create a certain chemistry, and at their best they can be as intellectually stimulating, even exciting, to students as the liveliest discussion or the most engrossing collaborative activity. They can also be an invaluable learning experience for the teacher giving them, because preparing and delivering lectures forces you to explain to yourself—before you try to explain to others—what you think is most important about your field and why it is significant.

Delivering your first lecture, and giving your first lecture course, can be a very intimidating process and will certainly involve a great deal of work. The onerous demands of preparing two or three lectures a week would be trying enough by themselves. But this difficult preparation coincides with teachers' efforts to master a form of activity that is, in many cases, entirely new to them. Few instructors have much if any experience in delivering lectures before they are called upon to offer a lecture course of their own. They must learn on the job.

Perhaps more than any other kind of teaching, lecturing puts the personality and the intellect of the teacher on display. It is, in a sense, a very personal kind of teaching, because in most cases it is you, much more than the students, who determine the nature of the classroom experience. You need to think carefully, therefore, about what kind of lecturing works best for you: what kinds of preparations you wish to make, what style of presentation you wish to use, and to what degree you want to encourage your students to participate in the lecturing process. You will probably find yourself experimenting with a number of different styles and techniques before you find the ones that are best for you. Most teachers remember lecturers they themselves encountered as students and will be tempted to borrow styles and techniques from those they admired. That is both natural and, often, helpful. But you should keep in mind that what worked for your teachers may not work for you. As much as in any other kind of teaching, lecturing needs to fit comfortably with your own temperament and personality.

Preparing a Lecture

A lecture depends heavily on the style of its presentation, to be sure. But it is, at its heart, a way of conveying ideas and information to your students. Even the most stylishly and engagingly presented lecture will be of little value if it does not contain real substance, and if it does not challenge students to think. The most important part of lecturing, therefore, is done before you ever enter the classroom: preparing and organizing your own ideas about your subject.

In preparing a lecture, you should think first of a question, or group of questions, you want to try to answer and of how the material you are considering in one lecture relates to the others you have given or will give. A lecture should not be simply a narrative or an assemblage of factual material. It should contain an argument, and the material you present should be organized to support and advance the argument. That does not mean that a lecture must be linear, with every passage moving relentlessly toward a single conclusion. There can be digressions, secondary arguments, anecdotes, jokes, and stories along the way. But when you reach the end of the class, students should have a sense of where you have taken them and why. Like a discussion, a lecture should not simply trail off when the bell rings. It should have a conclusion that draws your argument to an effective end and, perhaps, points ahead to what is coming next.

In structuring your lecture, keep in mind that you are speaking to an audience with very particular needs and expectations. They will want to know how the contents of your lecture fit in with other elements of your course—readings, papers, class discussions. They will want to know how each lecture follows the one preceding it or leads into the one following it. Most of all, they will want to take notes; and to do so effectively, they will need to be able to follow your argument easily and to recognize what is most important about it. Your lectures can be flamboyant, idiosyncratic, speculative, or fanciful. But whatever else they are, they should also be carefully and transparently organized. The central points need to be emphasized, and repeated, so that students are always clear about why you are covering the material you have chosen. (Repetition is usually something to avoid; but in lectures, repetition—particularly repetition of critical points—can often be valuable.) Without clear and explicit guidance, students will spend much of the class puzzling over what is important and how to take notes rather than listening to what you have to say.

Putting together a lecture, especially when you don't have very much experience at it, is a daunting task. It is not the same as writing a paper, an article, or a book. Unless you are lecturing on something that you yourself have researched extensively, an opportunity that will arise relatively infrequently for most people, you will have to rely on the work of others. You should feel no obligation to be wholly original. There is no reason for hesitation in borrowing material, even ideas, from articles, books, even other lectures—although you should not borrow specific language, and you should give credit to others when you are echoing particularly distinctive ideas borrowed from another source. When you are preparing two or three lectures a week over the course of a term, you will need all the help you can get; and the synthetic efforts of other people can often be of enormous value to you. Obviously, when all is said and done, a lecture should reflect your own ideas and interests and should not simply duplicate someone else's work. But those ideas and interests, more often than not, will have their origins in what you have read by others; and your lectures will inevitably reflect that.

Once you have decided on the topic and the broad argument of a lecture, spend some time reading or rereading material on your subject that you think is interesting and useful. If the subject is relatively new to you, you will probably not have time to read extensively; look for works that have already synthesized material on your topic, or that summarize the state of a field, or that fit your subject into a larger narrative. Take notes on the material and, as you are doing so, begin imagining how you will put it together for presentation to your class. When you have done enough reading (or when you have run out of time to do any more), begin organizing the material.

A lecture should not be simply a collection of facts, but even in such largely abstract fields as philosophy or linguistics, it should not be entirely conceptual either. Most students require concrete examples and illustrations to make arguments seem vivid and persuasive to them, and in most lectures you should be sure to have appropriate material available to support or illustrate your argument. Quoting from contemporary statements and documents—the more vivid and dramatic the better—is one good way to give concrete form to an argument. Another is to tell an illustrative story or to create a hypothetical example. Visual aids—images, films, charts, outlines, and other visual and audio aids (mostly now presented digitally through PowerPoint and other such programs) can do a great deal to add substance and detail to your lectures. Experienced lecturers are always on the lookout for bits of material—passages of text, humorous or dramatic stories, personal anecdotes, newspaper or magazine articles, scholarly papers, interpretive or synthetic essays, audio and visual material—that might help enrich or enliven their lectures.

When you find such material you should be sure to file or record it in some way (preferably with your lecture notes) so that it will be available to you when you return to a lecture topic. Striking a balance between illustrative material and the argument the material is meant to advance is one of the most important tasks you will face.

Lecturing from Texts, Notes, or Memory

One question all lecturers confront early on is what kind of notes will work best for them. Should you write out a full text of your lecture and have it in front of you in class? Should you simply make an outline or notes, and, if so, how extensive should they be? Should you speak without notes, and, if so, how should you prepare yourself for doing so? Making such choices will require you to think about, or discover, what works best for you. Each approach has advantages and disadvantages.

Many lecturers write out full texts of their lectures, and there are a number of good reasons for doing so. Writing a lecture out is the only way to be entirely sure you have worked through exactly what you want to say and how you want to say it; even the most extensive notes may leave you with some knotty problem unanticipated and unresolved and force you to struggle to deal with it while standing before your class; a finished text will require you to make such decisions in advance. Writing out lectures is also valuable in helping you fit your presentation into the time available. Once you have figured out how rapidly you can comfortably speak (which for most people is between two and three minutes per double-spaced page), you can use your written text to gauge the length of your lecture and adjust it to fit the time you have.

Another advantage of writing out lectures is that they provide you with protection against some of the vicissitudes of teaching. All instructors have bad days, when they are tired, distracted, ill, or for some other reason not at their best. Delivering a lecture can be extremely difficult under such circumstances, particularly if you are depending heavily on your memory and imagination to do so. Having a text in front of you can be an indispensable crutch on days when you lack the creative energy to do it on your own. Finally, writing out your lectures can be very useful in future years, when you return to a course, in providing you with a full record of what you have done and a starting point for doing it again.

But there are also disadvantages to written texts. Some lecturers can stand in a classroom, read a polished text, and sound as though they are speaking informally. But many others find it impossible to read a text without sounding formal and stilted and remote. If you cannot read a text smoothly and engagingly, and if you cannot comfortably digress from it or adjust it as you go along and as ideas occur to you, then you probably should not have one in front of you or, if you do, you should try not to read it. Written texts can also be addictive. They can tempt instructors to give the same lecture again and again, year after year. Stories of professors teaching from yellowed lecture notes are staples of academic mythology, but there is enough truth in them to serve as a warning.

For lecturers who feel uncomfortable with a written text, or who do not think it is worth the time to prepare one, a combination of an outline and notes often serves many of the same purposes—and sometimes serves them better. If your outline is sufficiently careful and detailed, then you may well realize many of the advantages of both a text (a full and well-developed structure and plan) and spontaneity (speaking to some degree extemporaneously and dynamically). Notes and outlines can be of any length and detail, of course, from a few notes on a single page to an elaborate document nearly as long as a written text. Indeed, some lecturers create notes that are nearly identical to a written text, but without fully formed sentences—to require them to extemporize to some degree as they deliver the lecture. Only experience will tell you how elaborate your notes must be to enable you to lecture at your best, or whether you will do better with a fully written text.

Finally, some lecturers prefer to lecture with no notes at all, or with such minimal notes that they are in effect speaking without any significant written assistance. This is a very risky approach for most beginning lecturers, but it can also be a very rewarding one, even if usually for more experienced teachers. To lecture successfully without notes requires a combination of a reliable memory—so that you will be able to recall your plan for the lecture as you go along—and an ability to be clear and articulate when speaking spontaneously. Lecturing successfully without notes requires at least as much preparation as any other kind of lecturing—and sometimes much more. However well prepared you are, you will still find yourself standing in a classroom with nothing to fall back on if your memory or imagination fails you on any given day. But if you find you are good at it, lecturing without notes can also be exhilarating for you and exciting for your students, who almost always notice when a lecturer is speaking extemporaneously and are usually very impressed when it is done well.

Delivering a Lecture

How you deliver a lecture will depend on many things: the size of your class, the character of your classroom, and most of all your own personal style. But there are guidelines that can help you decide how to present your material whatever the circumstances.

Some are obvious. Speak loudly and forcefully (using a microphone if necessary in a large room), both to ensure that everyone in the room can hear you and so that you do not seem tentative or unsure. If you are a first-time lecturer, you will certainly be nervous. But you can obscure a great deal of your own anxiety simply by speaking emphatically and clearly. Look directly at your audience as much as possible, and do not gaze only at one part of the room; avoid keeping your eyes glued to your notes, and avoid gazing at the ceiling or the floor or the wall or out the window.

Don't speak too fast. Even if you are running out of time, be sure to speak in a deliberate and unrushed way. Remember that students are taking notes and will be unable to do so effectively if you are rushed. If you have to, discard material (you can often use it later), or simply cut the lecture short (you can finish it next time). The best way to avoid rushing to finish a lecture, however, is to prepare it carefully to fit the time available to you. Don't speak in a monotone. Change your inflections and even your pace as you move from one kind of statement to another. And finish on time. It is both irritating and inconsiderate to your students to keep them late. Many of them will have other classes or obligations.

The physical conditions under which you lecture are also important. You will probably have little control over the character of the classroom in which you teach, but you should do your best to make certain that it meets a few minimal conditions. Obviously, your classroom should be large enough to accommodate your students so that everyone has a seat;

ideally, there should be at least 20 percent more seats than there are students. But the room should not be too large. A very big lecture hall for a small class creates a strange and disheartening atmosphere for students and teacher.

If you use a text or substantial notes, you should have a lectern on which to place them. Spreading your notes out on a table top makes them hard to see, forces you to spend too much time looking down, and can distract your students. If you plan to use the blackboard, make sure it is accessible and large enough and that there is chalk and an eraser. Make sure the room is adequately lit. Students will be very discouraged if they have trouble seeing the blackboard or their own notes. Finally, if you are using audiovisual or computer aids, make sure the room is equipped to handle them.

Although the most important purpose of a lecture is to help students learn, there is no reason it cannot also be entertaining. Even the most abstract and theoretical subject can be made more interesting to students if from time to time you digress from your central argument and throw in stories, anecdotes, and even jokes. The more engaging your presentation is, the more students will pay attention to its substance. But be careful not to overdo it. A few jokes and anecdotes can be very helpful; too many might lead students not to take you as seriously as you would like, and even to dismiss you as an entertainer rather than a teacher.

A difficult question is how much of your self you should put into your lectures. Should you tell personal anecdotes, recount personal experiences, and describe personal circumstances? If you feel uncomfortable talking about yourself publicly, then of course there is no need to do so. But an occasional personal story, assuming it is interesting or amusing and is in some way relevant to your subject, can humanize both you and your lecture. Do not, however, allow a lecture to become the occasion for elaborate explorations of your personal history.

There are other techniques that some lecturers use to help make their points. You can distribute documents, maps, charts, or tables to students as they walk in so that you can discuss detailed information without having to take valuable time presenting it. (You can also present the same material through images, or simply the blackboard.) You can write important names or terms on the blackboard so that students will have easy access to them (and their spelling). You can write an outline of your lecture on the board or project it with a computer to help guide students through your spoken presentation. (The minds of even the most dedicated students wander at times; an outline can help students reconnect with the lecture if they have temporarily drifted away.)

In the end, however, the success of a lecture depends on its content, and on your ability to deliver it convincingly. There is no single formula for doing that. Some lecturers pace the room and lecture in an animated way; others remain relatively still. Some are witty and humorous, others serious. Some use a great many visual aids, and others use none. The only things that all successful lecturers have in common are being clear and articulate, being organized, and being engaged.

Encouraging Student Participation

A lecture need not be a passive experience for your students. At the simplest level, the act of taking notes is itself an active involvement with your material, which requires students to summarize what you are saying and make choices about what is important. But many lecturers encourage students to participate in more direct ways. When your class is relatively small, it is easy to combine lecturing with discussion—to move in and out of your own presentation by asking students questions or eliciting their reactions. Even when the class is large, a lecturer can sometimes use Socratic methods to draw students into a discussion or simply solicit questions from the students.

As in any other class, your physical movements can make a big difference in a lecture, particularly if you are trying to draw students into a discussion. If you normally stand behind a lectern in order to see your notes, move away from it when you are engaging with students, to signal to them that the relative formality of the actual lecture is giving way to a more informal exchange. If you are standing behind a large table, walk around to the front of it, sit on it, and even walk into the aisle to address students who are asking questions or are responding to yours.

Keep in mind that in a large class, especially in a very large one, many students will be nervous when they ask or respond to questions. Be careful not to embarrass them, even inadvertently. Never make fun of a student's comment; don't laugh at anything your students say (unless what they say is intended to be funny); don't encourage anyone else to laugh at them either. Humiliating a student in public is something no teacher should ever do, both because it is an abuse of your authority and because it will virtually ensure that the student in question, and many others, will never speak in your class again.

When to encourage student interventions is an important issue, and one you should think about carefully before you begin to do so. Some lecturers encourage students to interrupt whenever they have questions. This might work well in a small class, in which the lecture is closely integrated with discussion. It can also work well in a larger class if the questions are not too frequent or distracting. But a lecture, more than a seminar or a discussion, is designed to present information and ideas to all your students; if a few voluble students begin interrupting frequently to ask questions that may be of little interest to the rest of the class, you will not be able to do what you need to do. You will also begin to lose the attention of the rest of the class.

Some lecturers try to save some time at the end of class for questions. That is not always easy to do, since you will often have difficulty fitting your lecture into the available period and will not have any time to spare. But if you have the time, encouraging questions at the end of your lecture will give students a sense that they can probe further into what you said without interrupting your presentation. If you are going to leave time for questions, make sure students know that in advance so that they can be thinking about what they might like to ask you as you speak.

Other lecturers begin each class by asking students if they have questions about the previous lecture. You might give them a minute or two to review their notes, but once you have established a pattern of soliciting questions at the start you will probably find that some students come prepared with them. You will, of course, need to shorten your lecture to offset the time spent on questions, but be careful not to allow questions to go on so long as to make it difficult for you to cover the material you have prepared for the day.

Still other lecturers incorporate student comments into the lecture itself by asking a series of questions of the audience, the answers to which will advance the argument of the lecture and also give students a sense of some of the intellectual questions that go into making a scholarly judgment. You should think carefully in advance about when in your lecture you wish to involve the audience, and where you want that involvement to lead. You should be careful, as well, not to allow the exchange with your students to stray from the points you want to illuminate or continue longer than you think is appropriate.

Student participation in lectures can be very valuable both to you and to them. But in the end, a lecture is primarily for the purpose of instructing, and whatever interaction you encourage should help you make the points you wish to make. In many other kinds of classes, student participation is to some degree an end in itself. In a lecture, it usually is not.

Most college and university lecturers will find themselves doing considerable lecturing whether they like it, or believe in it, or not. Giving a good lecture is, like most other teaching, a combination of art and craft. It provides you with many opportunities for creative expression, for imaginative presentation, and for projecting personal charisma. But even if you are not a naturally gifted lecturer, even if you feel you lack the intangible talents that can make lecturing a kind of art, you can deliver successful, highly effective lectures if you prepare carefully and work over time to find a style of presentation that is both comfortable for you and engaging to your students.

5

Student Writing and Research

The research paper or independent project is often the part of a course that students remember most clearly and from which they derive the most lasting benefits. That is because it is usually the part for which they are themselves most fully responsible and in which they can best pursue interests of their own.

In some courses—and some disciplines—independent projects are impractical or inappropriate. But in many others, the curriculum can and should include a research paper as an integral element. Obviously, though, it requires the same kind of careful planning you should give to any other important part of your teaching. If treated as a casual afterthought, it can become a confusing burden to students. It can also become a consuming chore for the teacher, who at the end of the term will face a flood of visits from panicky students searching desperately at the last minute for topics, followed shortly thereafter by the dismal task of evaluating an imposing pile of dreary papers. (Providing insufficient guidance for students undertaking a daunting and, for many, unfamiliar task can invite plagiarism as well.) But if integrated and planned carefully, the research project can become an invaluable extension of the course and lead to a greater appreciation of the subject. Most of all, it can help students develop vital skills and assume ownership of the learning process.

Relating Independent Projects to Your Course

If you decide to include a research paper in your course, you will also have to decide whether you want it to supplement or complement the rest of the curriculum. In other words, do you want the project to explore topics that you do not intend to cover but consider significant, or do you want it to reinforce topics that you already plan to address?

Both approaches have their advantages. A *supplementary project* is more challenging because it enables students to examine issues and material they will not otherwise encounter in class. As such, it places a premium not just on researching and writing a paper, but also on finding a way to define a topic beyond the scope of the course, which some students may find exciting but others may find intimidating. Of course, if desirable, you can minimize the anxiety by providing a list of possible topics, either broadly or narrowly defined, for those students who prefer less autonomy.

A *complementary project* enables students to pursue topics that are directly or closely related to the central themes of the course. As such, it may stimulate class discussions, deepen understanding of important issues, and permit students to pursue familiar topics with a degree of confidence and knowledge. This approach makes it easier for you to identify clearly what research or other materials students should use. But it also makes the papers less fully their own, denies them the opportunity to pursue subjects of personal or professional interest outside the parameters of the course, and makes it less likely that they will produce truly original papers.

It is not always necessary for you to choose between these two approaches. Consider giving the choice to those who will have to do the work. Let less confident or ambitious students select complementary topics, perhaps from a list you have put together. This will also accommodate the diversity of interests and backgrounds in your course. Let more confident and ambitious students—or those with strong preexisting interests—find and define their own supplementary topics, with or without your explicit guidance. Whether you want to weight the relative value of the different types of research projects is an option to consider, although it may complicate how you calculate the grades.

Guiding Students into Independent Projects

Students who intend to write a traditional research paper of their own design may need to learn the critical difference between a "subject" (an area of interest) and a "topic" (an issue or question that is arguable and manageable in terms of time and resources available). A student may, for example, have an interest in race relations in modern America; but that is not, of course, a suitable topic for a paper. The differing portrayals of the Watts Riot of 1965 in newspapers with primarily black or primarily white readerships, on the other hand, is a good topic that a student with access to a strong library can probably handle.

Students may also need to know that a successful research paper does more than present information—it also offers an argument that is neither unsupportable nor self-evident (as in "The Battle of Waterloo was a decisive moment in European history"). Quite simply, the thesis is the backbone or foundation of the paper. But formulating a coherent argument is often a difficult task for students. To assist them, require a short written proposal (or prospectus) well in advance of the date the papers are due. That will encourage students to begin thinking about their topics and the arguments they would like to make. It will also give them, and you, a chance to see if their ideas make sense when committed to paper. You can return their proposals with written comments, meet individually with students to discuss their topics, or distribute the proposals and have the class collectively offer suggestions.

Above all, many students—perhaps most—will need your help in recommending sources. In some cases, you may have a great deal of advice to offer. If so, provide guidance but do not overwhelm the students or prevent them from making discoveries on their own. It is, after all, their project. In other cases, you may have little expertise because you are unfamiliar with the topic. If so, do not try to disguise the fact but instead offer general guidance about print indexes and electronic databases. You can also identify helpful secondary works and scholarly journals, whose citations and bibliographies may contain valuable references.

Finally, do not feel as though you must do it all alone. Encourage students to speak with reference librarians, most of whom are eager to offer assistance and share information about their collections. It is also possible to use the Internet to locate and contact the authors of relevant works, who are often willing to reply to polite and reasonable inquiries. Remember that an appropriate topic requires available sources. Therefore it is essential that, as students begin to devise and define topics, they receive guidance so that they will develop a practical sense of research possibilities. If suitable sources do not exist or are not accessible—

a problem best discovered sooner rather than later—then it is time to revise the topic or select a new one.

Traditional and Multimodal Composition

If a full-scale, independent research paper does not seem appropriate for your students or your course, other kinds of written work can serve some of the same purposes. Traditional composition can take many forms. The *primary source essay* can give students experience in the use of written and visual sources. Have students select (on their own or with your input) a single text, or several, for close analysis. In literary fields, that might mean making use of whatever critical theory you are encouraging them to master. In history and other more empirical fields, it may mean asking them to consider the origins or impact of the text. In such cases, you might ask students to consider some or all of the following questions in preparing their essays:

- What was the viewpoint, motivation, potential bias, and intended audience of the author or artist?
- In what social climate and context was the cultural product created?
- What was its intended "message"? How effectively was it presented?

Encourage students to reinforce their arguments with evidence from class notes, assigned readings, or other sources.

The review essay is another type of writing assignment. It takes different shapes in different disciplines, but typically assumes one of two forms. The *contextual review* asks students to choose (either on their own or from a list you provide) a book, film, play, or other cultural text that had some impact on its age or has subsequently come to seem representative of its time to later generations, such as Betty Friedan's book *The Feminine Mystique,* the musical *Hair,* or Jean Renoir's classic film *The Grand Illusion.* The students then analyze the meaning and measure the impact of their selection by examining it closely and combining their general knowledge of the period with information gleaned from contemporary reviews and later criticism, biographies of or articles about the creator, or other sources. You might provide them with models for this kind of paper (which they will likely find unfamiliar) by sharing examples of successful efforts from previous classes. You might also provide published examples—retrospective or commemorative essays on the anniversary of a book or film, for example, or on the death of a writer or artist, which sometimes appear in serious magazines or newspapers.

The *critical review* allows students to assess the value of a significant scholarly or literary creation (or a related collection of such works). You might have students prepare a review based solely on the text. Or you might require them to use other reviews from scholarly journals, popular periodicals, and major newspapers as benchmarks. This is in some ways a less challenging assignment, and, particularly if they are reading other criticism, it may encourage students to substitute, wittingly or not, the ideas and opinions of others for their own. But it does help introduce students to the world of scholarship. It can also help demystify academic debates and reinforce the contested character of most scholarly work.

Here are some other types of writing assignments that you may find well suited to your course. They are not exclusive. In other words, there is no reason you cannot use a combination of them as you see fit.

Policy memos often work well as short complementary assignments in some disciplines. They are equally effective as preparation or closure for in-class activities like debates, discussions, and simulations. If you are discussing a particular historical, political, or even literary controversy in class, encourage students to write a short essay (a common length is one page) staking out a position on the issue. By removing the need to develop an original thesis, you permit students to concentrate on building a persuasive argument, with logical assertions and relevant evidence from whatever sources you have provided or identified. The students can then transfer that skill to other assignments that demand more independent initiative on their part.

Personal journals (also known as reading logs or diaries) are running commentaries on reading or other course work, which students keep throughout the term. At some point you should collect these journals, if only to ensure that your students actually keep them, and you might consider giving them a formal grade. The value of such assignments, however, is that it forces students to write regularly and, ideally, think seriously about what they are learning. To help you assess and reinforce the note-taking skills of your students, you may want to have the journals

contain lecture notes and reading summaries as well. Reading the journals may then provide you with a window into how students comprehend class lectures and discussions.

Oral histories can be a valuable and exciting project in many courses.
But make sure that students do not confront the assignment unprepared.
Help them become comfortable with the interview process, perhaps by
demonstrating interviewing techniques yourself or by having them interview one another in class. (A good published resource is *Doing Oral
History,* by Donald Ritchie.) Advise students not to organize their paper
around the interview; it is a source, not a subject. Suggest that they first
create an outline based on secondary research and then use the primary
information from the oral interview to confirm or contradict the written
record. Ask students to compare the different types of sources they use.
Have them assess critically the strengths and weaknesses of both scholarly versions of events and the personal memories of participants or contemporaries when they conflict. Keep in mind that at many institutions
oral history falls under the category of "human research" and may require permission from the appropriate office or committee.

"Minute" essays have become increasingly popular. They are low-
pressure, in-class writing assignments that give students a chance to
react to a question or issue raised in a lecture, discussion, or reading.
You can use the short essay to gauge student comprehension of a lecture, jump-start a discussion, provide closure to an activity, or probe to
see who has done the reading. You can give as little or as much feedback
as you like, and students get the opportunity to hone their writing skills.
Some instructors distribute "blue books" to the class at the start of the
term. The students then write all of their essays in the blue book, which
the teacher periodically collects, evaluates, and returns.

Finally, multimodal assignments using "new media" forms and
sources have gained wide acceptance in recent years thanks to technological advances that have become widely accessible. Using programs like
PowerPoint, Photoshop, Dreamweaver, and Flash, instructors and students can create hypertext essays with links to images, documents, or
sites on the Internet. Other possibilities include audio documentaries,
video blogs, image poems, and photo essays, which offer new and exciting ways to share information, voice opinions, express feelings, and promote interaction between the consumer and the creator, the audience

and the artist. Often the varied forms also magnify the emotional and intellectual impact of the work by facilitating multiple points of entry and exit.

Multimodal assignments do not negate the need to teach proper writing. On the contrary, the basic principles of effective composition remain important. But bringing "new media" into the classroom may enable students to take a more active and collaborative role in the process of creation. Used properly and selectively, it can also lead to a better understanding of the strengths and weaknesses of written, visual, or audio modes of communication. And it can facilitate critical analysis as well as give students a better sense of the multimedia world that they—and we—increasingly inhabit.

Above all, remember that no single assignment, whether traditional or multimodal, works well in all situations with all students. Each has its own particular advantages and limitations. First, decide what skills you want the students to acquire, what assignment will engage them, and what type of composition will stretch—but not overwhelm—their abilities. Next, determine what will best fit the content and format of the course. Then pick the assignment—or combination of assignments— that best meets those criteria.

Single or Multiple Assignments

If you decide to require writing outside of class time, you will need to decide how many papers to assign. The decision should depend on how central writing and research are to your course, and how much other work you expect of your students during the term.

Assigning one large paper allows you to assume, if you wish, a more active role in the various stages of creation, from requesting outlines and supervising drafts to holding conferences and permitting rewrites. It also gives students the opportunity to undertake a more substantial and potentially more rewarding learning exercise than a series of shorter essays would afford them. But a single major research paper may also overwhelm weaker students, whose needs may not become apparent until too late.

Assigning several smaller essays allows you to provide, if you wish, more feedback over the course of the term and to vary the types of writing required. It also reduces the pressure on any one grade and prepares students for activities and discussions you have planned. But it may reduce their chance to revise and polish a significant piece of writing, and it may also reduce your opportunity to guide them through the process. In the end, more writing opportunities may result in a less challenging and rewarding experience.

Naturally, other options exist. For example, you could assign a short essay in the first half of the term and a longer paper in the second half. This approach has several advantages. For one, it gives you the opportunity to evaluate the writing ability of your students at an early juncture and determine what sort of assistance they will need from you. For another, it gives students the opportunity to learn your expectations and test some of the skills that they will have to demonstrate later. For example, you might initially ask students to analyze a single primary source or scholarly article in a short essay if you eventually plan to ask them to incorporate several similar sources in a substantial research paper. You may also want to have the students create portfolios of their writing so that you can evaluate a body of work that represents sustained effort and assign a single grade that reflects incremental improvement.

Setting Standards and Deadlines for Written Work

Regardless of the type of assignments you decide to make, you need to give students guidance about what you expect from them. State and explain your expectations and standards early, clearly, and firmly; while some flexibility is appropriate, try to stick to your guidelines as much as possible to ensure that students take them seriously, especially if the paper is the basis of a subsequent discussion or activity. If you plan to use a grading rubric (see Appendix C), share it with the students so that they can see the criteria you will use to evaluate their work. Consider giving the students a checklist (see Appendix C) as well so that they can see what you expect them to do before they submit the paper.

The length of an assigned paper depends on many things: the number of papers you are assigning and the amount of other work you expect; the ability and experience of your students; the kind of paper or papers you are asking them to write; and the norms of your institution. For a substantial research project, it is reasonable to expect students to write at least ten pages and—depending on the school, course, and students—sometimes up to twenty-five pages. The longer the paper, the less time students have to do other work. So in general avoid assigning a paper of twenty pages or more unless it is the main focus of the course, as in a research seminar.

Other kinds of papers can range from one or two pages to ten or fifteen. Whatever you decide, make it clear to the students at the beginning of the term. Make it clear, too, if you have a particular format you wish students to use. It is not unreasonable to insist that all students use a computer. Beyond that, consider whether you want students to provide footnotes, endnotes, or some other formal method of citation; whether you want a bibliography; and whether you want a summary or abstract at the beginning or the end. Any such requirements, of course, create an obligation on your part to explain how to meet them. Footnotes, endnotes, and bibliographies, in particular, need considerable illustration (and, where possible, access to a good style guide, such as *The Chicago Manual of Style* or Kate Turabian's *A Manual for Writers of Term Papers, Theses, and Dissertations* or *A Student's Guide for Writing College Papers*. Software programs like Endnote and word processors like Word 2007 provide significant help in ensuring that you are using the correct form).

Think carefully about when you want the paper to be due. Explain early in the term and repeat later what your policy is for late papers. If you are willing to grant extensions, state a clear and consistent policy and do not deviate from it. When a student asks for an extension, establish a new due date (and keep a record of it). If you plan to penalize lateness (and you should if you expect students to respect the deadlines), clarify what the penalties will be and under what circumstances they will be imposed—then make no exceptions. Penalties are usually appropriate if a student hands in a paper late without having arranged for an extension, or if a student does not adhere to a new due date that you have jointly established. In general, some flexibility on due dates is usually a good idea, since most students are juggling many obligations. But make sure that the flexibility is not arbitrary, that you have made your rules clear.

Almost all students are highly grade conscious, and how much a paper weighs in the calculation of the course grade will have a considerable impact on how much time and attention they devote to it. If you think the papers in your course are important, weight them heavily. But whatever you do, stress from the start—preferably in the syllabus—how much the papers will count.

Supervising Written Work

Setting guidelines means more than announcing expectations and requirements. It also means helping your students plan and execute their projects. If you are assigning a research paper based on primary sources, for example, spend class time talking about what a primary source is and how to use it. If you are assigning a review essay based on secondary sources, give an example of what such an essay might look like. Then help students learn how to identify and locate sources. If it is logistically possible, and if you suspect your students have little previous research experience, arrange for a tour of your institution's library. Many students today believe that research begins and ends with the Internet. Often they are physically unfamiliar with the library and intellectually unaware of how to make the best use of the resources it provides.

Guiding students through their projects is not a one-time exercise. Return to the subject of the papers frequently during the term. To the degree that your own schedule permits, encourage or require students to schedule individual conferences with you to discuss their work. Such conferences allow you to monitor their progress and help them with any problems they may encounter. Finally, urge students to help one another. For example, devote some class time to having them work in pairs or comment collectively on a particular project. Or divide the class into editorial groups in which students engage in peer editing and offer peer critiques throughout the term. The more collaborative learning you encourage in class, the more collaborative learning you will see outside of class.

Grading Written Work

Even under the best of circumstances, grading papers can become a long and tedious ordeal. But how you respond to them matters to students, who will often remember your comments long after you have written them. So try to grade the papers in a reasonably comfortable place at a relatively tranquil moment. Do not rush. Allow sufficient time for reading and grading.

But try to return papers relatively quickly, within a week or so of the due date. A long delay may diminish the value of your critique, because by then the attention of the students has shifted to other tasks. In the end, quality matters more than speed when it comes to grading written work. If a reasonable delay in returning papers is the price of careful evaluation, it is probably a price worth paying.

First, determine whether the assignment justifies extensive comments. If it is of relatively little value or comes at the end of the term, it may not warrant a large investment of time. But if it is a major paper—and especially if students have the option to rewrite it—then it is best to offer as much guidance as possible. Comments are most useful when students can put the advice to good use shortly after receiving it. Second, consider handing out a style sheet (see Appendix C) to your students that provides numbered or coded rules on grammar, punctuation, quoting, and so forth. This will save time because you can use short codes in place of lengthy comments or repetitive corrections. Finally, remember that you need not be a copy editor—fixing every mistake of grammar or punctuation may drive both you and the student to despair. And it may distract you from more important issues of analysis and interpretation.

Written comments should include a blend of compliments, criticisms, and suggestions for improvement. Even the most disappointing paper should receive at least some praise, if deserved, while even the most accomplished paper should receive at least some suggestions for how to address the topic more effectively. Sometimes it is more important to stroke the ego of a weak student than a strong student. In any event, lead with a compliment. Then offer criticisms and suggestions for improvement. Try to conclude on a positive note—it will make students more receptive to the other comments. Avoid false compliments, as students can often sense condescension or hypocrisy, and avoid excessive criticism. Be relatively direct and sparing—you do not want to overwhelm the students or drive them to disregard all of your comments.

Above all, let students know that your criticism reflects not contempt but confidence in them, that it shows how seriously you take their work and their potential for progress. Never be sarcastic or derisive or dismissive. If you offer suggestions for revision, focus on a few of the most important problems and ask the student to concentrate on addressing them. No one can concentrate on correcting or improving ten things at once.

Writing the comments on a computer will not only save you time in composing but will ensure you have a copy for yourself. If you opt to write comments by hand, either because they are brief or because you find using a computer difficult, make them legible and keep some record of them in case students later have questions. Fairness matters—in perception and reality—when assigning grades to papers. Undoubtedly, you will evaluate papers on the basis of a combination of factors, including whether they have a clear argument, solid structure, ample evidence, careful analysis, strong logic, and smooth style. But for many students the difference between an "A" and a "B" paper is not obvious. Therefore you may wish to devise an explicit grading rubric (see Appendix C) and share it with the students in advance so that they can develop a better idea of what your expectations and standards are. It may also make the grading process easier and more consistent for you.

Of course, grading is an imperfect science at best. So always keep in mind that you are not evaluating students, you are evaluating their work. Do not unfairly penalize a student who has somehow irritated you. Nor should you unfairly reward a student whom you may particularly like. Some teachers take steps to ensure that they do not know the identity of a paper's author when grading the work, which is a bit of a hassle. But the principle is sound, because it suggests how difficult it often is to separate personal feelings from professional judgments.

Be suspicious of your immediate reaction to a paper that comes on the heels of a wonderful or dreadful one. A good paper may suffer unfairly in comparison to a terrific one; conversely, a poor paper may benefit unfairly in comparison to a horrible one. If you find papers that trouble you in some way, or about which you are truly uncertain, place them in a separate pile and return to them when you have read all the others. Having a better perspective on the full range of student work will give you a better sense of how to handle the problem cases.

Disagreement over grades is virtually inevitable. Do not discourage students from challenging you. But require that students wait at least a day before bringing a paper to you with questions or complaints. This will allow them time for pause and reflection. It will also allow tempers to cool. Second, if the complaint seems reasonable, offer to reread the paper—but reserve the right to lower as well as raise the grade. You will find that, upon reflection, many students reconsider their request.

Revising Written Work

Most teachers write and rewrite as a matter of habit. But for many students, the paper that they submit represents their first and last draft, with perhaps a quick application of the spell-checker and a few final cosmetic corrections. This approach to writing has a number of negative consequences. First, it means that the paper you receive is usually not their best effort, which leaves you with the unpleasant option of bestowing either an undesirable or undeserved grade. Second, it represents the loss of a significant learning opportunity—and renders superfluous (at least in a direct sense) any comments or corrections you may offer.

It is therefore a good idea, if circumstances permit, to let students revise major papers after you have read and graded them. In general, the more important the project—the greater the investment the student has in it—the stronger the case for allowing revision. A chance to rework a paper gives the author the opportunity to benefit from, and respond to, comments from you or peers.

If you choose to permit rewrites, make the offer optional and universal from the start. But place a clear ceiling on how much they may improve the original grade so they have an incentive to do as well as they can the first time. Encourage them to provide a short statement about weaknesses they hope to address in the rewrite. Set a firm deadline for the final submission and urge or compel those who wish to rewrite their papers to meet with you so that you can determine whether they understand your comments and know what they need to do.

Under the best of circumstances, allowing students to revise creates more work for them and for you, although there is no need to write extensive comments or repeat earlier criticisms. Nevertheless, teaching students how to revise is a valuable life skill. As we know from personal and professional experience, good writing is rewriting, and we should do what we can to encourage the habit.

Preventing, Detecting, and Acting on Plagiarism

By virtually all measures, plagiarism is a growing problem. According to a recent study, more than 70 percent of college instructors encounter at least one incident per year. At the same time, many students have come to believe that information on the Internet is public property and represents common knowledge that does not require citation. Some are willing to purchase papers from online services or borrow papers from friends. Others are content to lift passages from published sources, whether on the Internet or in print, and use them without proper attribution.

Few academic infractions are more serious than plagiarism. It cuts to the heart of what scholars seek to do, which is to advance the state of knowledge in original ways. Yet few academic subjects are more difficult than plagiarism for students to understand and for teachers to tackle. Part of the problem is that raising the issue implies a lack of trust in the students. And part of the problem has to do with the fact that many students simply do not understand what plagiarism is, how to safeguard against it, or why it should matter if they never intended to steal the words or ideas of others. Nevertheless, if plagiarism is a matter of concern to you—and in our view it should be—it is incumbent upon you to address it clearly, directly, and proactively.

PREVENTION

The first step is to explain your motives—to state why you take plagiarism seriously and why it is important to give credit where credit is due. Emphasize that it is not a matter of trust—it is a matter of respect for their work and the work of others. The second step is to state what the penalties or consequences are from both you and your institution. Emphasize that you will impose them if necessary. The third step is to define as precisely as possible what plagiarism is. An excellent source of information and ideas is www.plagiarism.org. If possible, provide concrete examples from real or fabricated papers. Here it is vital to stress that intent is irrelevant and in any event impossible to determine to any reasonable degree. If a work contains language, ideas, or materials borrowed without proper attribution, it represents plagiarism, regardless of whether the individual meant to do it.

Most students easily understand that copying constitutes plagiarism. They grasp that it is wrong to submit a paper that someone else wrote or that contains passages lifted verbatim from other published or unpublished sources. But some do not see that submitting the same paper in two different courses is, in effect, self-plagiarism unless one gets the permission of both instructors involved. Stress to students that not only should the work they submit be their own, but it should be work created specifically for your course.

More difficult to explain is how to deal with language, ideas, and information derived from other sources. Students generally understand that when they use language (three or more consecutive words) that is not their own they should place it in quotation marks and provide a citation. But do not take it for granted—state it in class and put it in writing. Even harder to explain is what to do with ideas drawn from other sources. Explain to students that borrowing an idea is not wrong, but they must ask themselves if they would have generated it on their own. If not, cite the source—whether or not they express the idea in their own words. Emphasize that paraphrasing does not remove the obligation to provide attribution, which will simultaneously buttress their argument and provide proof of research. Finally, students should understand that it is not necessary to cite information that is common knowledge (as opposed to expert knowledge) or easily referenced in standard sources (as opposed to specialized sources). But these are tricky standards and elusive distinctions. In the end, the best rule to share with students is "when in doubt cite it."

At the same time, you should take reasonable precautions as the instructor. Try to design assignments that are, to the best of your knowledge, unique to your course—then vary them from term to term or year to year. Ask students to respond to specific issues raised in lectures or labs. Frame research projects around special topics and sources that you have identified. This may reduce the scope of student initiative and independence, but it will also reduce the scale of plagiarism. Finally, build in checkpoints that will deter plagiarism. Require that students provide a prospectus, outline, or notes—even a first draft, if only as circumstantial evidence that the final product represents original work. But these checkpoints may also improve student planning and diminish student anxiety, which can sometimes lead to bad choices. Always remember that with plagiarism, preventive measures are worth far more than a punitive cure.

DETECTION

You will almost certainly confront an actual or potential case of plagiarism at some point in your career. When the moment arises, you will essentially have several options, not all of them good. Ignoring plagiarism is unacceptable because it compounds the likelihood that the student will do it again, which in turn merely shifts the burden to another teacher. Going to the library or the Internet, reviewing the sources the student used, and trying to determine whether plagiarism is time-consuming and difficult.

More appropriate is to invite a student whom you suspect to have plagiarized to your office and ask him or her some questions about the paper. What source was most helpful? What was the most difficult part of the paper to write? What exactly does a particular assertion mean? What information was most surprising or disturbing? If you receive vague or incoherent answers, you can pursue the matter further. Of course, the student may realize that you are probing for a reason and react in a hostile or defensive manner. Unfortunately, this is sometimes unavoidable and, if you are wrong, you may have to apologize. But you can and should note that you acted in good faith because you care deeply about the problem of plagiarism.

Another option is to use technology to your advantage. Select a suspicious phrase or two from the paper in question and see what a Google search finds. If the student has lifted material from Wikipedia or another popular online encyclopedia, Google will flag it quickly. Another alternative is to submit the paper electronically to an online site like Turnitin .com, which offers subscriptions to individuals and institutions. It will immediately search for text matches with published materials on the Internet and unpublished materials (mainly other student papers) in its large and growing database. Turnitin.com will then list the matches and provide links to the sources in question. SafeAssign, a feature available on Blackboard, a widely used course management software program, works in a similar fashion and offers instant reports that indicate the degree of duplication. To download free plagiarism-detection software designed by Professor Louis A. Bloomfield of the University of Virginia, visit http://plagiarism.phys.virginia.edu. Students may also wish to use these services to check for proper citation and safeguard against accidental plagiarism.

Both Google Books and books on Amazon that allow it make possible searching through books fairly efficiently. They may provide you with useful information and may deter some plagiarism if students know that you are familiar with these services. Nonetheless, in the end the decision as to whether further investigation is worth the time and effort will remain with you.

ACTION

Never act on a case of possible plagiarism unless you are confident that you are on firm ground. First, gather and scrutinize the evidence. Make copies of the student's paper (or at least the relevant sections) and the sources that he has made improper use of in your opinion. Then review the policies of your institution in regard to plagiarism. Perhaps you are not free to render a decision on such charges. Perhaps you must refer such matters to an administrator or a faculty-student committee. But if you have the right and choose to confront the student, strive to remain calm and objective. Give him the opportunity to explain his side of the story before you rush to judgment and punishment.

Always act discreetly and deliberately. Remember that an accusation of plagiarism is a serious matter that, if sustained, can have a major impact on the student's future. You may wish to deal with different cases in different ways. For example, you may choose to treat a student who has cited material insufficiently or inaccurately more leniently than a student who has submitted a paper that she did not write or that includes material without attribution. But bear in mind that you have an obligation to your discipline and profession—not to mention the other students—to remain faithful to your policies and principles. If you have preached against the evils of plagiarism and then uncovered a serious violation of this central rule of academic life, it is your responsibility to confront and report it to the proper authorities, regardless of the consequences for the student in question.

Sharing Student Research

Research papers and serious critical essays are the most original things most students do in secondary and higher education. Scholars undertake such projects in the expectation that other people will read them.

Encouraging your students to do the same has considerable value; so try to make the work of your students available to the entire class—and perhaps even to people outside the class.

The simplest way to allow students to share their work is through an informal activity, such as an unstructured discussion. Over the course of the term, occasionally steer discussions toward topics or projects on which students are working. Ask the appropriate individuals—with advance notice—to report on their research. Consider setting aside a class, or several classes, in which students can give short reports on their work—perhaps including examples of their research or samples of the texts they are reviewing. Set strict time limits, however, and enforce them.

Peer review panels also provide an effective way for students to present their research and learn what their classmates have discovered. Form panels composed of several students working on related topics. Then have individuals present brief summaries of their work and comment on the work of their fellow panelists. Other members of the class can, of course, join in the discussion. Web pages on the Internet or course pages in a managed site like Blackboard are another alternative. Require or request that students upload their papers, or abstracts of their papers, to a password-protected site. Then assign them to the rest of the class as optional or mandatory reading. If desirable, have students post comments and invite the authors to respond.

Making student work available to others has many benefits. By sharing individual discoveries with the whole class—and, possibly, the larger intellectual world beyond—you treat your students as scholars and give them a greater stake in their research projects. You also broaden the amount of information and number of viewpoints to which they are exposed. In a sense, you enable them to become part of the community of scholars.

Doing research and writing papers is, in many disciplines, the most important and most challenging form of learning. Students take much more pride in work they have created themselves than they do in any other kind of work. They also discover a form of learning that no classroom experience can replicate. It may not always be possible to incorporate research and writing into your courses. But when it is possible, make an effort to do so and emphasize its importance. Giving students the experience of creation has great potential rewards.

Testing and Evaluation

Tests and examinations are not usually a student's, or a teacher's, favorite exercise. But fair tests, thoughtfully constructed, can be not just a valuable tool of evaluation but also a tool for learning. Preparing examinations, and preparing your students for examinations, is an important part of most courses.

It is, of course, not always necessary to give tests or exams. Some courses use papers or projects as the basis for evaluation instead. In most cases, however, some kind of exam will be appropriate. And in many cases, it may be required by your institution, whether you like it or not. It is, therefore, important to know how to design exams that are effective, fair, challenging, and creative. The goal is to construct tests that give students a chance to show what they know—not what they don't; that cover a range of material or skills so that all students have a reasonably equal chance of success (not just those who have mastered one particular skill or body of knowledge); and that force students to think rather than merely recite facts.

Both strategic and tactical issues lurk behind the creation and implementation of every test, from the simple surprise quiz to the elaborate final exam. The time to think about these matters is not a few days or even weeks before you plan to give the exam. The best time to do it is before the course begins. That way you can decide how to relate the material you cover in your course with the expectations you will have of your students when the exam period arrives.

Needless to say, you should not—to use a term often associated with college entrance or AP examinations—"teach to the test," although in this case, of course, any test to which you teach will be one of your own devising. But it does make sense to consider exams an integral part of your course.

Keeping Students Informed

Whatever kinds of tests you give, ensure that your students are fully informed about them. Announce the dates of exams well in advance. Remember that like you, students have busy lives and need to plan their schedules. Some institutions set exam dates centrally. But if the timing is up to you, do not reschedule an exam casually. In the face of a "vocal minority" who may want a change, a "silent majority" may expect you to hold firm. Before you decide to make a change, consider whether it will serve all—or at least most—of your students, and whether it will prove overly disruptive to you.

Provide complete information well in advance about the content and format of any exam. The goal of a test is to reinforce skills and to find out what students know—not to catch them by surprise. Give them a rough sense of how much the exam will draw on readings, lectures, discussions, or research. Making old tests available to all students will help them visualize the format, force you to rework previous efforts, and eliminate the possibility that some clever individuals might gain an advantage through access to "bootleg" copies. (Sometimes, of course, there is good reason to use questions from old exams again, so think carefully about whether you plan to do that before releasing copies to your students. If you do plan to draw from old exams, however, it is better to draw from tests several years old, not from ones that students currently on campus may have taken.) Above all, early disclosure will force you to think about the exam in advance and avoid writing it in a rush the night before.

Make the value of the test clear. If it will constitute a large proportion of the final grade, stress that fact and create conditions that will help students prepare for it—such as review sessions or a reduced reading load in the days leading to the test. If it is worth relatively little, make sure that students keep their eyes open to other, more important, assignments or evaluations down the road.

Planning for Examinations

One of the first things to decide is how many tests you plan to give, and when you plan to give them. Frequent tests or quizzes often help weaker students master manageable amounts of material. They also allow you to monitor the progress, comprehension, and effort of the students—particularly if you suspect it has flagged when it comes to doing the assignments. But multiple tests consume precious class time as well as student and teacher energy.

The most common pattern of testing in colleges and universities is the traditional model of a midterm and a final. In some places, it may also be the mandatory pattern. The model has many advantages. It requires minimal class time. It forces students to synthesize large amounts of material. And it allows you to use the exams to turn your attention—and theirs—to broad themes and ideas. One drawback is that the final is the only opportunity for students to demonstrate that they have learned from their mistakes on the midterm. Another is that many learners have difficulty absorbing large amounts of material. A possible compromise is to begin with relatively frequent evaluations and gradually extend the period between them. Of course, this is generally possible only if you are teaching a year-long rather than a semester-long course.

But exams are not only a factor in students' lives. They are a factor in yours. Unless you have a large course with teaching assistants, you will have to write and to grade the examinations. Therefore it is important to think carefully about your own schedule and responsibilities. Do not create impossible burdens for yourself.

When to give exams is also a significant issue. In some cases your school or department will make the decision for you by establishing times when you must test so as to not conflict with other courses. But if the decision is yours, keep several things in mind: If possible, choose dates that reflect natural breaks in the material you are covering. Also select dates that do not conflict with, or come too near to, other likely student obligations in your course and outside it. Try to avoid dates of schoolwide importance (such as major athletic or social events) as well as those of countrywide importance (such as tests like the LSAT, MCAT, GRE, etc.). If many of the students have similar schedules, consider when the other courses are likely to have exams. And, again, do not forget about yourself. Since you are probably teaching several courses, it is a good idea to stagger your workload as much as possible, especially since you may want (or have) to evaluate the exams rapidly.

Give thought as well to where the students will take the exams—in class or at home. Each site has advantages and disadvantages. An *in-class exam* forces students to master the material so that they are prepared to present it rapidly under the artificial constraint of time pressure. It tends to reward those who have prepared carefully, who react well to pressure, who form their thoughts quickly and write rapidly, and who know how to anticipate the questions you will ask. It tends to penalize those who have spent less time preparing or who take longer to formulate or write answers.

A *take-home exam,* by contrast, permits students to write their essays under a somewhat less artificial constraint, such as a twenty-four- or forty-eight-hour deadline. It allows them to think more carefully about the questions you ask them, to pay more attention to organization and writing, and—if you permit it (as you probably should, since you will have no way to enforce a prohibition)—to consult sources. A take-home exam is less a test of memory and more a test of thinking and writing.

A take-home exam offers benefits and costs. The good news is that you will receive typed answers and will not have to worry about deciphering the handwriting of your students who, like most of us, rarely write by hand any longer. You can also apply regular standards of grammar, punctuation, organization, evidence, and thought. The bad news is that students may be tempted to spend less time preparing, thinking that they can retrieve the information they need during the day or so they have to write the exam. Some students may also receive unauthorized assistance, which is extremely difficult to monitor or prevent. Finally, most students will certainly write longer essays than they would in class.

It is, of course, possible to combine the two approaches, with an in-class component that includes relatively specific questions designed to test student knowledge of the material you have presented to them and a take-home component that includes longer essays or problems that will test their ability to frame and support arguments. Another compromise is to distribute a larger group of exam questions in advance while informing your students that only one or two will appear on the exam. Students will then have to prepare broadly but not indiscriminately.

Preparing Students for Exams

Some teachers assume that because students have taken tests before, they need no preparation to take them now. But all exams are different. Students who have taken multiple-choice or standardized tests for many years may have no idea how to write an essay on an examination. If you are concerned about how well your students are prepared, survey the class well in advance of the first exam to see what experiences they have had; or give them an assignment that will allow you to determine how well prepared your students actually are for the kind of exam you intend to give them.

Perhaps choose to use part of a class period to offer some practical tips on how to write a timed essay—perhaps by giving students a sample question and asking them, either individually or in groups, to outline a response. No matter what, explain to them that they should always think first (even if for only a few minutes) and organize their thoughts before writing their essays. Another way to help students prepare for exams, and to make the process less intimidating, is to provide models of successful essays or good responses to short-answer questions so that students can see more clearly what you expect.

The last step in preparing students for the exam is to use the test itself to guide them into their work. Always include written directions on your exam, particularly mechanical requirements such as how many questions students should answer, how they should label their essays, and how much time they should devote to each section. Keep the instructions moderate in length—you do not want the students to waste a great deal of valuable time reading instructions. But they should provide a clear guide to the exam and the expectations you have of your students.

Handling Missed Exams

It is inevitable that from time to time students will fail to take, or be unable to take, your exams. Illness, family emergencies, oversleeping, schedule conflicts, and a host of other reasons—good and bad—will leave you with the difficult task of deciding how, and whether, to allow students to make up for their absences.

On this issue, your department or your school may have policies that will determine your options. Make sure you know them. If you are permitted to establish your own policy, try not to reward those who miss exams out of negligence or penalize those who have legitimate reasons for their absence. Keep the following rules in mind:

- Insist that students who anticipate an unavoidable conflict inform you well in advance.
- If you plan to give a makeup exam, establish the date in advance. Make it as soon as possible after the original exam so that students do not forget the material or learn too much about the original exam. Choose a time that will not conflict with other courses. To deter students from electing to take the "makeup option," perhaps select an inconvenient time, such as early morning, evening, or even a Saturday (if you are willing and it is permitted by your institution).
- Revise the original exam with care. Replace multiple-choice or short-answer questions that will obviously leak to absent members of the class. But do not necessarily discard an essay question that is well constructed and addresses a major theme of your course. Instead, change the wording somewhat or reformulate it with a slightly different slant.
- If you have distributed a group of essay questions in advance from which you were planning to select one or two for the exam, recycle the used questions or select new questions—the choice is yours.

Constructing an Exam

Recall that the goal of the exam is to evaluate how well students have learned the themes, skills, and content that you consider important—not to trick or "catch" them. Exams can consist of several different kinds of questions in many different combinations. You should select the combination that best fits the objectives of your course and the abilities of your students.

The *essay question* is the most challenging and, in many ways, the most valuable kind for students in most fields in the social sciences and humanities. There is no substitute if you want your students to engage in higher-level thinking. A good essay question will not just stress memorization of facts. It will take a significant theme from your course and ask students to develop their own interpretation or response using information that they have encountered in class and in the readings. It should also provide them with both structure and room for initiative. Finally, a good essay question should produce a range of responses that reflects the varied abilities and perspectives of your students.

Use verbs like "analyze," "assess," "compare," "contrast," "explain," and "evaluate" to signal an open-ended, higher-order question. Avoid verbs like "list" or "describe" that will generate responses with little analysis, unless you intend to use them in conjunction with those that require critical thought. Choose questions that are neither too broad nor too specific. Be sure students can answer them in the time allotted. Steer clear of multipart questions unless you clearly identify each component.

Perhaps the most familiar kinds of essay questions are those that ask students to respond to a statement or passage of text. You might present them with a quotation from another scholar, or from a primary source, and ask them to respond to the claims the author has made. Another option is to construct a quotation of your own and ask students to respond to it. But make sure that any quotation raises a question clearly and unambiguously. A good essay question should not require arduous deciphering.

Some teachers give students primary source documents (or excerpts) to analyze and integrate with their answer to a question. Ask how the documents shed light on the question. The addition of document analysis will reinforce critical thought, give weaker students a prop for their essay, and provide stronger students with the opportunity to generate more sophisticated syntheses.

Always reread the questions after you have written them. Ask yourself if the language is too broad or vague, or subject to interpretations that you do not intend. If you are at all uncertain, ask colleagues if the question seems to "work." If you have teaching assistants, give them a chance to react to the questions; they, after all, will be grading at least some of the responses to them, and they are, after you, the people most familiar with the material in your course. If you are a teaching assistant yourself who has been asked to draft exam questions, confer with your fellow teaching assistants.

The *multiple-choice question* has a bad reputation. Many consider it a crutch for lazy teachers or lazy students, who want to focus only on rote memorization. But multiple-choice questions, when crafted with care, can test the ability of students to apply analogies, synthesize interpretations, analyze texts, and sequence events. When used in conjunction with essay or short-answer questions, they can help provide broad and balanced coverage of the course content. They can also add an objective component to your test, highlight possible flaws in your teaching, and give poor writers a chance to improve their grades.

A multiple-choice question consists of a stem (the body of the question before the choices are presented), the incorrect responses (sometimes known as distractors), and the correct answer (known as the key). Use clear language in the stem. Avoid double negatives and obscure terminology. Emphasize important ideas, events, or individuals, not trivia. Use the same number of responses in any group of questions; five is the norm. Make the responses similar in format, length, and grammar; do not introduce unnecessary complications for students. Avoid "all of the above" or "none of the above" responses unless it seems absolutely necessary or appropriate. Last but not least, proofread carefully to be certain that the question makes sense and has only one right answer.

Some instructors design multiple-choice tests so that the most difficult questions come at the end of the test. This helps reduce the likelihood of students' panicking early on when confronted with a question they cannot answer. It also means that slow readers will have a better chance of getting through the test without getting hung up on hard questions at the start.

The *short-answer question* is a good compromise between the essay and the multiple-choice question. It allows you to test for factual knowledge and critical thought without placing hefty writing burdens on the students or onerous grading burdens on yourself. It is also less limiting than a multiple-choice question. Ideally, it should be used in combination with other types of questions to create a broad and balanced exam.

Here are several types of short-answer questions (see Appendix D):

- *Identifications,* or IDs, typically require that students provide a brief synopsis (a few sentences) of a person, character, event, idea, or term. Insist that they also describe why the ID is significant, and that they relate their description to a theme of the course or the lecture in which the ID appeared.
- *Clusters* consist of lists of ideas, items, or events. Ask students to place the material in the proper order and explain why the sequence makes sense. Or provide a list of terms and have

students put them in pairs and explain the relationship between the elements in each pair.

- *Source-based questions* can be particularly useful in terms of skill development. Present students with a written (chart, graph, cartoon, or document), visual (video clip, slide, or photograph), or audio (music or other recording) source; ask students briefly to identify whichever of the following are appropriate to the source: the author, intended audience, relation to larger themes, and point of view.

Avoiding Cheating on Exams

Just as you must be alert to the possibility of plagiarism in written assignments, you need to be alert to the possibility of cheating on exams. Most students are honest and will avoid temptation, but some will inevitably act improperly, whether out of cunning, fear, weakness, or some combination of all three. Nevertheless, there are steps you can take to make cheating more difficult and less successful.

Certain kinds of questions, such as multiple choice, are easy targets for cheating; students can easily look at the work of others while taking the exam. Even on essay exams, students might bring crib sheets into class or arrive with material already written in blue books. Help prevent this kind of cheating by giving two different sets of multiple-choice questions, randomly distributed among students. And of course it is a good idea to monitor exams actively—and make sure students know you are doing so—to discourage wandering eyes. To avoid situations where students try to substitute their "prepared" blue books for those you distribute, pay close attention at the start of the exam. Also, try not to repeat the same essay questions year after year.

Grading Exams

Once you have created and administered the test, you will have to grade it. Do not procrastinate. The task will not become easier if you delay. And if you wait too long to grade exams (other than the final), the opportunity to use them as a learning instrument will disappear as both you and the students move on to new subjects and concerns. So try to return the test as soon as you can, preferably within a week if possible.

Establishing a set of standards or criteria for essays before you begin will help you to grade quickly and fairly. It will also help students understand why they received the grade they did since you may not have the time or inclination to write extensive comments on their exams. Some typical criteria for essay questions include the following: Does the essay contain a clear and well-developed thesis that answers the question directly? Does the essay demonstrate critical and/or original analysis or thought? Does the essay support its thesis and analysis with substantial and relevant evidence from appropriate sources? Is the style of the essay appropriate? Is it well organized and well written given the time constraints? Is the essay marred by major errors that detract substantially from the argument?

There is no one right way to grade an exam. You might choose to break the exam into its component parts and grade each separately—for example, do multiple-choice sections for all students first, followed by short-answer and essay sections. Skim several exams so that you can get a feel for what an average paper looks like and what grades are appropriate for what level of performance. Try to grade comparable essays in a group. That is, if students had a choice between questions A and B, first evaluate all of the A essays and then all the B essays. Write the grades in pencil at first or keep them on a separate sheet of paper so that you can change them if necessary. Sometimes an essay will, on an initial reading, appear inordinately good or bad in comparison to what has come just before it; your evaluation may change after you have read more. Give yourself frequent breaks so that your mood does not affect your scores.

Consider evaluating the overall quality of the exam at the end, reflecting on the grades you assigned to the separate sections. You may wish to alter the subjective grades slightly in order to give each student the overall grade you think he or she deserves. If time allows—and often it will not—write comments on your exams, but not extensive ones. For essays, make concise references to the criteria or standards you set. For short-answer or multiple-choice questions, simply indicate what the correct answer is if the student has made an error. A general principle for providing comments is to write enough so that if a student brings you the exam later and asks you to explain the grade, reading your own comments will remind you of why you evaluated it as you did. As with commenting on papers, be careful to comment on exams respectfully and, as much as possible, encouragingly. Do not spare students criticism when they have made mistakes or done poorly; but try to include some encouragement or praise if there is any basis for it. And never write comments that will seem condescending, scornful, or nasty. Write as if the students you are grading are doing their best, even if you suspect that is not the case.

Some institutions have a policy of not returning exams. But if you do return them, try to return them as soon as possible. But do not do so until you have had a chance to reflect on what the exam has told you about what your students have learned—or not learned. When you do return the exam, spend some time in class discussing any problems or trends you have diagnosed (unless of course the exam occurs, as it often does, at the end of the term and after the class has dispersed for vacation). It often helps to distribute an especially good answer to a question (with the student's permission, and preferably anonymously) and lead a discussion of why it was so successful. But there are dangers to this approach. If your model essay is dramatically better than the norm, there is a danger that it will intimidate some students; if it is not, it may annoy students who think their essays were equally good or even better. You can avoid some of these dangers by preparing and distributing a model essay you have written yourself, although the problem of possible intimidation may be even greater in that case.

Keep grades confidential. Do not leave graded exams out in the open for students to retrieve, since that will give students a chance to see the grades of others. (It may also tempt students to steal good exams by others for future use.) The federal government has mandated that the records of students remain confidential through the Family Educational Rights and Privacy Act (FERPA). Many states have passed similar laws, and most universities have codes of their own. But whatever the rules or policies of your institution, never discuss grades with anyone but the individual involved.

Remember, finally, that the fault for a disappointing performance on your exam may lie neither in your students nor in the stars but in the exam or you. Reread the questions carefully after grading the exam and ask yourself whether the way you framed or constructed the questions was responsible, at least in part, for the problems students had. Consistent gaps in student knowledge or skills may indicate that either the exam was faulty or that you failed to present the course material as well as you had thought or hoped. Reevaluating what succeeded and failed after the fact is a vital part of constructing and reconstructing exams. It is also a vital part of helping you evaluate your own teaching.

Teaching Science Challenges and Approaches

Science teachers at the college level face many of the same challenges as instructors in the humanities, arts, and social sciences face. Students in the sciences often have trouble integrating the various fragments of knowledge presented to them and fail to see connections between theory and practical application, between the classroom and the "real world." As a consequence, they tend to forget what they have learned shortly after the final exam. This is not surprising since the human brain stores information only in short-term memory when it does not comprehend the long-term usefulness of the knowledge.

But science teachers also face challenges that are specific to their fields. For one, many students without a strong background in science arrive with a serious case of "science anxiety," which conditions many of them to expect struggle or failure. For another, many science courses feature both lectures and labs, which offer students an opportunity to engage in active learning and critical thinking but also require special preparation, organization, and management strategies on the part of the teacher. Finally, and perhaps most importantly, many science instructors, even more than instructors in other fields, have had relatively little previous training or preparation in the art of teaching even if they have significant experience in the laboratory.

In graduate school, many students in the sciences—unlike their counterparts in the humanities or social sciences—work as research assistants, not teaching assistants. Most of their time is spent in the lab assisting their adviser or pursuing their own research. Graduate courses in science fields usually do not devote significant time, if any, to pedagogy. Moreover, in research-intensive universities teaching is often secondary to research, particularly when it comes to a tenure decision. As a consequence, science instructors typically and rationally devote their energies to designing experiments, publishing papers, and submitting grants for research funding. This focus often comes at the expense developing new teaching methods, improving existing lecture materials, or running an effective teaching laboratory.

This chapter addresses the special and specific needs of science instructors. It begins by exploring course objectives. Then it examines how to teach introductory and advanced science classes, including active learning techniques and reading assignments that go beyond the textbook. Next the chapter discusses the lab experience as well as other ways to engage students, including fieldwork, case studies, and independent research. It concludes by discussing various ways to assess students' learning.

Course Objectives

As you begin to plan a course, develop specific objectives for the entire semester. Before the term begins, decide what the general content of the course must cover and then plan specific lectures that collectively will provide students with the knowledge they need. Of course, the objectives will vary depending on the backgrounds of the students and what their expectations are for the course. Remember to consult with your colleagues (unless you are, for instance, the only physics teacher at your institution). If you are teaching an introductory course that serves as a prerequisite for an advanced course, find out what background knowledge that instructor expects students to have. If it is an advanced course, explore what topics and skills were emphasized in the introductory course.

Then determine what objectives you wish to emphasize in each lecture. Think of the big picture you would like to present to students and the message you hope they will take home with them. This will help you select the details and determine the order of individual parts of each class session. As you start to outline individual lectures, recall that it is important to link material to prior learning and show how it is applicable to larger issues or problems so that students will efficiently retain the knowledge in their "memory bank." For instance, during a lecture on pharmacological therapy of high blood pressure remind the students of how a healthy body maintains normal blood pressure and the pathological mechanisms that lead to blood pressure abnormalities. Together, this background information will help put things in context. It will enable the brain to create a new "folder" or direct the new information to an existing one named "blood pressure regulation." Similarly, if you are a chemistry teacher, highlight examples of chemicals covered in your class that are components of household cleaning products.

To assist this process, construct what is called a "concept map" (see Appendix E). This is a hierarchal diagram that shows and connects pieces of information, starting from a major concept then expanding to details of its various aspects. The main concept, for example, could be the structure of a mammalian cell. In this case the next layer of information detail is represented by dividing the topic into the cell membrane and the cytoplasm, followed by expanding on the individual constituents, biochemical makeup, and function of each component. Start with basics, and then move on to more advanced knowledge. Go from the general to the specific, from big ideas to smaller ones, from the concrete to the abstract (for example, from a piece of metal to atoms). Use the "concept map" approach to highlight the specific place of a given classroom session within an entire course, similar to the "you are here" arrow often seen in a shopping mall location map. This structured pattern of information flow helps the brain consolidate the learned material and store the new information, leading to more meaningful learning rather than simple memorization.

Science Courses: Introductory and Advanced

Wide varieties of students often take introductory science courses. Some may major in science and plan a career in a scientific field, while others are there simply because they are required to take your course for a degree in a nonscience major or as a prerequisite for another, more advanced course. A good teacher must cater to both camps and attend to their different needs, motivations, and interest in the topic. The teacher's role is to excite all students about the material being presented and make it both accessible and comprehensible. But often this is not easy. Start each lecture with a summary of its content and the concepts to be illustrated. Include in the introduction a summary of background information presented in the previous lecture. This helps the students shift to second gear to absorb and process new pieces of knowledge.

It is vital that a teacher understand the challenges that face first-year college students who take introductory science classes. Many factors may affect the performance of students at this stage of their college education. Introductory college science courses are often very comprehensive and address a broad scope of content. Too broad a course does not give students a fair chance to absorb information readily. College science teachers sometimes expect too much in regard to students' background knowledge of the subject. This expectation is usually based on seeing a list of the science courses the students took in high school and their grades in these courses. Yet the reality is that high school courses are often based on memorization of facts rather than analysis and assimilation of different pieces of knowledge. Grades in high school might also be significantly inflated.

A particularly challenging aspect of teaching science is what is commonly known as "science anxiety." This anxiety is usually planted during the high school years. Many high school students fear taking science classes due to a perception that they are difficult and might hurt their overall GPA. Unfortunately, this notion is sometimes echoed and amplified by students' advisors and counselors. "Science anxiety" is further heightened by the sudden switch from requiring memorization to comprehension. Research supports a relationship between the preconceived difficulty of science and the perceived ability of students to learn and perform well in college-level science courses. As a science teacher you must serve as a good role model to help change the general negative attitude of students toward learning about science. This requires working hard to transform their mindset to get them genuinely interested in science rather than considering your course a necessary evil. Assure students that you are aware of their fears and will do your best to provide a smooth transition and make science education an enjoyable experience for them. Show how the specific knowledge they will gain applies to their daily lives and ability to perform various physical and intellectual functions and tasks in their contemplated professions. Students often become excited by learning how the information in their science textbooks was derived, and how important pieces of scientific discoveries have resulted from serendipity or from simple observations by someone with a curious mind—someone who is sometimes an undergraduate student like them!

Unlike introductory courses, advanced courses should include both core information and up-to-date knowledge, which changes at a rapid pace in most scientific fields. This requires the teacher to keep up with recent developments in the field and to differentiate between foundational information provided in textbooks and cutting edge knowledge recently published in specialized science journals. While advanced textbooks, particularly those that are frequently reprinted and updated, offer essential basic information, assigning carefully selected recent review articles or individual papers related to the topic are excellent tools for delivering current knowledge (see below). Establish an appropriate balance between the two types of information. This balance depends on the level of the course and the background of students.

At the same time, excite students in advanced courses by telling them they can expand their knowledge in a particular area if they opt to pursue a career in scientific research—and give them a sense of what a career in science may be like. Furthermore, make them aware that most important pieces of scientific knowledge are the products of various disciplines in science. For example, information on gene therapy comes not only from the field of genetics, but also from new advances in understanding the pathological mechanisms underlying a given disease, drug-delivery technology, and so on. Try to highlight the importance and uniqueness of this concept of a scientific melting pot. Advanced science courses should also emphasize the development of analytical skills, something that is best done through the following activities and strategies.

Teaching Strategies

Active learning can and should play a major role in a science class. In particular, it can help students assimilate current information with previous knowledge and apply it toward problem solving. The many merits of active learning discussed in other chapters of this book are equally important and directly apply to teaching science. Active learning builds complex understanding rather than simple memorization of facts and enables students to apply their knowledge to new contexts. It also helps students develop logic and appreciate the power—as well as the limitations—of scientific research. Active learning, moreover, makes them aware of what types of questions could or could not be answered with reliability and confidence.

Active learning can take many forms. To see whether students understood the information you just presented in a lecture, ask them to come up with examples or applications of what they learned. Put students in command. Another strategy is to divide the class into cooperative groups that work together throughout the semester. Dedicate the last ten minutes of each or some lectures to active learning exercises. Start by asking each group to summarize the main elements of a given scientific concept. Ask probing questions to engage students and invite their participation. Good questions often start with "how," "what," or "what if." Follow up by giving them an example that requires a specific application of a general concept. End the session by having representatives from each group summarize their conclusions to the entire class. Have the groups rotate their spokesperson from class to class.

Here is an example involving the case of bacterial resistance to antibiotics. The opening question may be about the cellular and molecular mechanisms that underlie this health-threatening phenomenon. Examples of follow-up discussion points may aim at testing students' knowledge about incorrect practices by prescribing physicians, hospitals, or patients that increase the incidence of bacterial resistance and how to avoid such practices. Ask students to discuss how a physician or a pharmacist should proceed in the case of a patient who has developed a bacterial infection that does not respond to a given antibiotic. Make constructive comments whenever you deem it helpful to jump in or offer concluding remarks at the end. Another example is teaching heat-resistant polymers. Ask students to come up with practical examples for utilization of these materials. This includes road pavement material and space shuttle external panels.

Of course, introductory science classes sometimes have hundreds of students. This makes a structured division of students into permanent cooperative groups chaotic when you ask students to change seats to join their designated group. A good and more practical alternative in this case is to form spontaneous cooperative groups of students in different class sessions. Form groups or pairs of students sitting near each other. Either ask for volunteers or choose individual students randomly to present the conclusions of their discussion to the class. Make sure you do not embarrass anybody who is not prepared to speak. Allow students the opportunity to pass their turn if necessary.

Teaching Labs

Laboratory sessions are an integral part of teaching science. Labs serve to demonstrate a concept or principle. They can also teach new skills or techniques, including illustrating how to use modern instruments. In more advanced science labs students learn how to design experiments, interpret their results, and draw educated conclusions. Most importantly, labs serve as an environment conducive to planting and nourishing scientific curiosity and appreciation of the nature of the process of scientific discovery.

A lab environment is also conducive to applying various techniques of active learning such as discussion groups and debate teams. By working in groups students become more acquainted with each other and with the concept of teamwork. Above all, labs are useful in providing students with hands-on experience in producing knowledge of the type they read about in the course textbook. This might stimulate the curiosity of some students to pursue a career in scientific research.

In most cases, labs are simply venues to prove and illustrate concepts that have been covered in a lecture setting. However, labs could also serve as a means of inquiry. This more stimulating variation involves giving students the opportunity to formulate a specific hypothesis based on background knowledge, develop a set of questions to test the hypothesis, and design experiments to address these questions. Following collection of data, students are taught how to analyze and interpret the experimental results. One exciting outcome of such an exercise is the anticipated difference in the experimental designs and conditions chosen by individual students or groups of students in planning and conducting their experiments. This variability leads to different, but complementary, sets of data and can pave the way for exciting discussions. Giving students a free hand to design and execute their lab exercise by no means relieves you of your role in providing background information and constructive directions. Do not stay away from the lab benches. Roam around to observe what the students are doing and listen to their remarks about different stages of the experiment. This will build confidence and offer reassurance to students. And it will provide you with useful material that will help you prepare to lead discussion at the conclusion of the experiment.

Do not teach individual lab sessions in isolation. Relate each lab to previous ones and to associated topics taught in the classroom. Connect the specific goals of each lab with those of the entire course and the general state of knowledge in the particular field of science. This approach places the information taught in both the lab and the classroom in a broader context. Start each lab session by explaining the specific goals of the planned exercise and its relevance to course content. List three to five concepts to be illustrated. Explain theoretical principles underlying the experiment, but do not turn the session into a formal lecture. Briefly highlight the practical steps of the experiment, particularly ones that are technically difficult or require an exceptional degree of accuracy. If necessary, demonstrate how instruments should be set up and any parts of the exercise you expect to be challenging to students. Emphasize the timeline of the experimental and discussion parts of the lab session, and what is expected of individuals and groups.

Always be present during the entire lab session, both physically and mentally. Never bring reading material or exams to grade during the lab. Walk around and observe the proper use of instruments and safe lab practice. Pay attention to group dynamics and progress in relation to the time allotted to the experiment. Answer questions. Ask questions. Compliment those who have shown progress in their experiment. Help others who are having difficulty. Intervene only when you notice serious problems. Convene the entire group to provide guidance if you sense general confusion or frustration related to instrument setup or a specific experimental step.

The closure of the lab session is at least as important as the experimental exercise itself. Now is the time to get students excited about science and illustrate the value of having individuals or groups contribute discrete pieces of information to the collective knowledge of the entire class. The outcome of this closing segment will play an important role in getting the students to look forward to the next lab session. Allow ample time for this group activity. Start by asking students to remind you of the goals of the lab activity and which theoretical principles it relates to. Review the results recorded by individuals or groups. Highlight consistencies and inconsistencies. Discuss possible causes of such variability without embarrassing the particular experimenters who obtained the odd results. If the exercise involves different assignments to different groups of students, engage the entire class in a discussion of how to put the various pieces together in order to synthesize scientific concepts and principles.

Prior to the start of the term prepare a clear, detailed manual for the lab. Lab manuals can be simply step-by-step cookbooks. This format suits lab exercises where all students must perform in the same way and expect a specific result. The manual should include the titles and dates of various lab exercises as well as their goals and relationship to course content. Include a description of methods of preparation of experimental reagents or animal dissection. Stress the calibration and proper use of lab instruments. Enumerate the individual steps of the experimental procedure. State specific outcomes for each experiment. In the next section of the lab manual spell out lab policy in terms of student conduct, for example, roles and responsibilities and hazardous or disruptive behavior. Define academic misconduct and its consequences, including cheating or plagiarism. Elaborate on the safe handling of lab reagents and operation of instruments and machinery. Incorporate a section on procedures to handle laboratory accidents or injuries, including emergency phone numbers and evacuation plans. Stating a grading policy for the lab session is of utmost importance since many students might not be familiar with what is expected of them. The policy should include how many points are dedicated to attendance, quality of performance and the produced experimental data, lab reports, understanding of concepts, and contribution to group discussion.

Before the lab begins, plan the timeline of various activities, such as your introduction and explanation of the planned activity, time allocated for the lab exercise, and discussion of the experimental results. If applicable, divide students into groups and assign roles and responsibilities. Check availability and functionality of experimental material, chemical reagents, lab instruments, and audiovisual equipment ahead of time. Nothing is more embarrassing to a lab instructor than switching on an instrument or adding a substance to a chemical reaction with nothing happening.

Now let us turn to the different types of labs.

Demonstration Labs. Such labs serve many functions. They are used to elaborate on important concepts covered in the classroom. They are also useful for illustrating an experiment or practical procedure that is not amenable to being done by the students, either individually or as a group. This might be due to the high cost of required chemical reagents, limited availability of lab instruments, or the potentially hazardous nature of the experiment. In this type of lab session the instructor takes the driver's seat. However, student engagement in the process is essential to attain the most effective learning. Without active involvement by students this exercise might easily turn into "another lecture" and will therefore lose its unique features and function. Ask students to comment on the importance of different steps of the experiment or formulate educated guesses of anticipated results. Seek volunteers to offer interpretation of the data resulting from the experiment. Pose a series of "what if" questions.

Virtual tools are particularly helpful in allowing students to learn lab lessons that require demonstration of experiments that might be hazardous (for example, a chemical reaction that yields explosive or inflammable products). They are also helpful in case of material that is difficult to obtain (for instance, cadavers) or in case of experiments that require days or months to complete, such as studying the effects of varying the chemical composition of soil on the size, color, and flavor of strawberries. Simulation models play a similar important role. You could use an electronic dummy to illustrate concepts of emergency medical care, such as cardiac resuscitation, the Heimlich maneuver, or childbirth. There are also simulation models for teaching proper wound suturing, dental care, and so on.

Hands-On Labs. These labs usually consist of students performing a set of experimental steps included in the lab manual and reporting on the results. Many undergraduate students look at such science labs as a "must do" chore. Students generally believe that the most important outcome is to produce the "correct" anticipated results and are therefore simply interested in finishing the assignment as quickly as possible. This attitude is unfortunately reinforced by the majority of instructors who grade the lab exercise according to how close a student's result is to what is "expected." This robotic performance by the students comes at the expense of analyzing critically the experimental results and relating them to the theoretical concepts learned in the classroom. It impedes intellectual stimulation and instills in students a fear of producing unanticipated results. Yet these "errors" are often essential for scientific advancement. Students will usually work in silence unless they have a technical problem, in which case they will ask for help. Very few will be proactive in asking theoretical questions or in engaging in discussions with the lab faculty, teaching assistant, or each other.

Open Labs. They are useful in case space or equipment is limited. They allow students to perform the lab assignment at the time of their choice within designated daily or weekly time periods during which lab instructors are available. This flexible arrangement better accommodates the schedules of students who have significant extracurricular obligations, such as families or jobs. It also caters to students with different intellectual abilities and performance styles, particularly those who need more time to complete a given task. The open lab system, however, does not work well for all students. It particularly allows for procrastination in case of students who are not highly motivated, which could lead to lab crowding toward the end of the week.

Inquiry-Based Labs. These labs aim at enabling students to develop good questions related to theoretical concepts and independently design experiments to address these questions. Students may work individually or in small groups. In dividing students into groups be aware that students have different backgrounds and are at various stages of preparation and scientific maturity. Take this into consideration when forming groups with mixed levels of expertise. What is particularly exciting about this independent approach to lab experimentation is the virtually unknown nature of the results to be obtained. This is due to students' individualized decisions on experimental design and parameters. There is no right or wrong answer as long as students can adequately justify their choices in how they designed their experiment. At the end of the lab convene the entire group for discussion of the experimental findings and what they mean. The nature of experiments will obviously be limited by available laboratory equipment and reagents.

Inquiry-based labs require developing certain problem-solving skills based on reasoning patterns. These are mental strategies or rules composed of *if/then/therefore* sequences of mental operations that enable one to assimilate learned information and derive conclusions independently. Thus, it is important to provide students with general guidelines for the process of scientific inquiry. This process starts by gathering observations, followed by formulating a hypothesis and testing its validity. Thus, start by asking students as a group to describe the background observations or information at hand. Ask them to identify gaps in existing knowledge and pose questions to fill these gaps. Better yet, ask them to formulate a hypothesis that underlies the questions to be addressed. Emphasize that as long as the hypothesis is logical, it does not really matter if the results of the experiments support it or disprove it. Either case lends itself to thought-provoking discussions based on reasoning.

From there let each student or group of students design their independent experiment to test the hypothesis using the reagents and instruments available in the lab. Ask them to outline the steps of the experiment, record the results, and think of their interpretation. It is very important to test their knowledge by checking whether they include all the important experimental controls, without which it would be difficult or impossible to interpret the data with high confidence. As a rule of thumb, each experimental group or additional step in the experiment must differ from the one preceding it by not more than a single element. For instance, if students plan to test the effects of a new chemical dissolved in alcohol on the boiling temperature of water, they must also test the effects of alcohol alone. Without this control it is not possible to interpret any measurable changes in boiling temperature as being due to the chemical under test per se. Students should also be familiar with the proper designation of independent and dependent variables: the concentration of the test compound and the boiling temperature of water in this particular example, respectively. Upon finishing their experiments gather all students for discussion of the results obtained by different individuals or groups. Stimulate discussions by asking which of the experimental results are for and which are against the proposed hypothesis. Ask if the overall set of observations should lead to postulating a modified or completely different hypothesis to be tested. Explain to students that this circular iterative approach is at the heart of the process of scientific investigation.

It is your role to entice students to become engaged in the process of inquiry and discovery. Remind them that experiments are the only way to unfold new scientific knowledge. Emphasize that this creative approach to lab experimentation is undoubtedly more exciting than simply reading in textbooks about knowledge that others have discovered. Share with them anecdotes of major scientific discoveries that were mainly derived from simple experiments combined with keen observation. Mention examples of paradigm-shifting discoveries in the laboratories of Nobel laureates, some of which were stimulated by observations made by an undergraduate student who joined the lab to gain first-time research experience or by a junior lab technician. Some of these were due to pure serendipity, such as forgetting to include a certain reagent in a chemical or biological reaction or inadvertently letting a reaction go longer than planned. You may not get all students excited about lab exercises, but you will undoubtedly motivate some. Relate the theoretical concepts underlying a given experiment to practical, real-life examples. Take the example of a lab exercise to determine the effects of salt on the melting temperature of ice. The concept that salt lowers the melting temperature of ice relates directly to what students living in colder parts of the world experience after a snow or ice storm, when they observe trucks spraying salt on highways to facilitate the melting of snow and to ameliorate slippery road conditions.

Other Approaches to Teaching Science

Reading Assignments beyond Science Textbooks. It is important to offer reading assignments, particularly in advanced science courses, that go beyond the textbook. Assign short but informative review articles as reading material in the beginning of the semester. For inexperienced students or those taking the course as nonmajors select articles in general or discipline-specific review journals that provide summaries of the background and state of knowledge in the targeted topic. Good resources for such review articles include *Scientific American* and *Science News*. The weekly science section in the *New York Times* often launches spirited debates about scientific issues. Articles with graphics and schematics are especially helpful in demonstrating concepts. Discuss with students the main concepts stated in the review and how the given field of science has advanced from one stage to another. Highlight turning points in acquiring knowledge in the subject matter.

Later in the semester choose readings from primary literature in the form of published papers that report on important scientific findings. Ask students to read and comprehend the content of the various sections of the paper (introduction, experimental methods, results—including graphs and tables—and discussion of the results). The main goal is to enable students to acquire advanced knowledge on their own. Exposing students to primary literature is vitally important for preparing them for careers where, ideally, they will keep abreast with the most recent developments in their field rather than continue to rely on textbooks. Nowadays science advances so rapidly that most textbooks are already outdated by the time they are published. Reading primary literature exposes students to the actual way in which scientific findings are introduced to the science community and to those who apply these published findings in their particular profession. It also makes students appreciate the incremental nature of progress in science.

This strategy closely parallels the recent push by the American Association for the Advancement of Science and the National Research Council to transform science education to facilitate the development of scientific skills such as critical evaluation of experimental methods and strategies, application of concepts, and putting pieces of information together to synthesize new knowledge or hybrids of knowledge. Try to select articles that report on exciting, paradigm-shifting research findings or discoveries that are intimately related to the educational goals and objectives of your course. A good and reliable source of papers for students who major in a given branch of science is multidisciplinary science journals that publish high-impact papers in various fields, such as *Nature* and *Science*.

Choose papers that include a clear background and are based on multiple approaches to answering and validating a set of important questions. Avoid papers that are heavy on technical details. These articles might cause confusion, which might lead students to miss the important concept addressed in the paper. Alternatively, select several papers published sequentially by a given prominent team of investigators to illustrate how they moved from one stage of knowledge development to the next. Perhaps locate an important scientific question that has been debated back and forth by two or more groups of investigators. Ask students to justify why they support conclusions made by one side over the other. This approach will strengthen the critical thinking and analytical skills of the students.

Of course, students must first learn how to comprehend and critique scientific literature. Such initial preparation will provide them with a solid foundation to build on and will make your mission throughout the term much easier. It is your role as a science teacher to get your students to appreciate that there are few "facts" or "constants" in our scientific knowledge. Examples of facts include that nothing is faster than light, or that adding together two identified chemicals always produces the same byproduct under constant reaction conditions. In the latter example, however, the "proposed" molecular mechanism by which the chemical reaction takes place is not a matter of fact. Our current knowledge of these mechanisms is limited by the sensitivity of available instrumentation, and is therefore subject to revision and refinement once more sensitive instruments or new technologies are invented. Making a clear distinction between "facts" and "the state of current knowledge" enables students to critique and analyze existing scientific information.

It is also important to familiarize your students with differences in the level of accuracy and reproducibility of various types of measurements that constitute scientific knowledge. Repeated laboratory tests of the biophysical characteristics of a new polymer designed for highway construction, such as its melting temperature, resistance to pressure, and so on, should yield results with low variability. The situation is not quite the same, however, in case of testing the performance and durability of this material in different highways. Here the results depend not only on the chemical and physical properties of the polymer, but also on the traffic patterns, geological composition, and geographical location of the test site, among many other factors. The same applies, perhaps to a more pronounced degree, in determining the correlation between the dosage of a given medication and blood level. Many factors influence this relationship, including age, gender, metabolic rate, diet, and other medications taken by different study subjects. Any of these variables could alter the rate of absorption and breakdown of the medication in either direction. Introducing students to the idea of data variability teaches them that they must assess critically what they read in the literature and not take the conclusions made in a single publication as a scientific dogma.

You may choose to assign a seminal paper in the field and ask students to critique the experimental design and evaluate whether the authors adequately support their findings. Ask each group of students to analyze and interpret one of the figures or tables in the paper, and then discuss their findings with their peers. This type of reading assignment could either be open-ended, or you may provide students with a specific list of elements in the paper you would like them to assess.

Take, for example, a paper that reports on the beneficial effects of a new medication in a patient population that suffers from high levels of blood cholesterol. Ask students to evaluate the quality of the sample of study subjects in terms of their number, health and medication history, age, gender, and ethnicity. Ask how one might improve the quality of the studied sample. Other questions to consider may include the following: Was an appropriate placebo similar in shape, color, and taste to the medication capsules used for proper comparison? Did the study include all necessary controls to validate data interpretation? What are the overall strengths and weaknesses of the experimental design? How appropriate is the statistical analysis of the data? What are the main conclusions of the published study? Are the conclusions made by the authors adequately supported by the reported data? Which piece of the data is most crucial in support of these conclusions? Which is the weakest link? What experiments would you design to gain more confidence in the interpretation of this particular set of data? How do you rate the paper in terms of its overall contribution to advances in the treatment of high levels of cholesterol? How do you compare the reported efficacy of the tested drug to that of cholesterol-lowering medications already available in the market? If you were one of the authors, what questions would you ask to help design the next study? Offer extra points to enthusiastic students who refer to the literature cited in the paper to gather relevant information to help formulate their critique.

Alternatively, assign a group of papers with the goal of comparing and contrasting instruments employed, experimental designs, findings, and conclusions. Put the student in the position to gather information that supports or negates the authors' conclusions. In this case, start by assigning different papers to individual students or small teams of students and ask them to provide a succinct summary of the various components of the paper. Then ask students to give a brief presentation to the class, with a short question and answer period. At the end have an open discussion by all students. This approach simulates what happens at scientific conferences where new and exciting research is presented and critiqued by other peer scientists. It is also very helpful in training students in public speaking skills. Alternatively, organize a poster session, a different form of delivery of information at scientific conventions. Another variation on the theme is to divide students into two groups to play the role of defense and prosecution in a trial. The two groups debate the merits and shortcomings of the assigned paper, respectively.

Still another, more advanced approach is to provide students with the tables and figures published in a selected paper and ask them to describe and interpret the data as if they were the scientists who conducted the study. After you receive the students' comments give them the actual text of the "results" and "discussion" sections written by the paper's authors and ask them to debate whether they agree or disagree with the authors' interpretation of the data.

Case Studies. Case studies are the best format for teaching students how to analyze information and apply it to a real-life situation. Take the example of constructing a new highway bridge. This task requires knowledge of the properties of various construction materials, anticipated traffic patterns during the day, and the average weight of vehicles that would utilize the planned bridge. One must also gather information about the geology of the construction site and regional climate conditions. All of these factors, and many others, are necessary for calculating the proper amounts and ratios of construction material, dimensions of the bridge, maximal allowable weight load, and so on. Students may be divided into groups, each of which would handle obtaining one of these pieces of necessary information. Discussion by the entire class should follow to help all students pull information together. More important, this type of exercise will show that the overall process must be iterative, where making decisions on one aspect of the project will depend on knowledge of another. This could be followed by an exercise in which the instructor changes one parameter and asks students to figure out the effects on other parameters. For example, what difference would it make if the bridge is designed for a highway in Minnesota compared to Florida where there are significant climate differences? Computer-based stimulations are very helpful in this regard. They offer the freedom and flexibility to effect gradual changes in one or more parameter to find out the effects on others.

A similar approach could illustrate to medical or pharmacy students the concept of drug-drug interactions. For example, consider the case of a patient who was prescribed two medications that accelerate or decrease the rate of metabolism or excretion of each other. What happens if one changes the dose and timing of the administration of each drug in either direction? What are the consequences of such interactions between medications in terms of their individual therapeutic efficacy or toxicity? How does the picture change if the patient has a compromised metabolism, excretion, and so on? What types of food potentiate or attenuate these interactions? What alternative medications could be used to avoid these undesired drug-drug interactions?

Good case studies have general criteria and attributes; most importantly, they must have well-identified learning objectives. They should be short and manageable within the allotted time. However, you could choose a longer case and divide it into various segments to be covered in consequent sessions. More stimulating are those cases that are contemporary and relevant to a specific component of the course or lab. You might select a controversial case that would stimulate debate, but do not go too far in this direction. Real cases are better than fabricated or generic ones. They provide a stimulating core context that students can identify with, particularly if you use a recent case that was widely publicized and debated. This approach provides an excellent opportunity for students to practice their problem-solving and critical-thinking skills. It also best prepares them for real-life situations in their future careers.

There are many variations on how to apply case studies in teaching science. These include presenting students with a video vignette followed by specific questions. You can also apply a debate or role-playing format. One setup that requires significant problem-solving skills involves providing students with details of the case ahead of time. This gives them a chance to search textbooks and recent literature for information that would help them proceed with their assessment of the case. Or perhaps assign specific tasks to individual students or groups of students. During discussion of the case students share the information they gathered and how this information addresses the case at hand. Determine what additional information is needed to gain more insight into the case. This approach sharpens students' ability to locate and assess relevant information and to work as a team. As always, be cognizant of your role as a moderator and facilitator of discussion, rather than being the one who solves the presented case. Keep the session stimulating and smooth flowing. Do not let certain dominating students manipulate discussion and intimidate those who are too shy or too intimidated to participate.

Science teachers who supplement their traditional lectures with frequent case studies face some challenges. Most importantly, careful and successful design and execution of case studies is more time-consuming than preparing for a conventional lecture. Case discussions also require certain personal attributes of the teacher, such as the ability to moderate and steer dialogue in the most productive direction. Also expect to face resistance by students who are used to formal lectures and are therefore unwilling to accept a new style of teaching and learning. Finally, some of your department colleagues or college administrators may challenge your choice of this modern way of teaching as opposed to more traditional methods.

Fieldwork. Incorporating fieldwork experience in a science course has many advantages. It makes learning more exciting, allows students to apply knowledge learned in the classroom, and gives them practice in integrating different bits of information. This brings the learning experience and its application closer to functional practice. It also trains students in the valuable skill of observation that is critical to sparking new advances in science. It trains them to question facts when they observe something that does not fit with the accepted norm or scientific dogma. Fieldwork demonstrates to students the very first steps in the process of discovery and assimilation of knowledge they will eventually read about in their textbooks. It also illustrates firsthand the importance of ensuring the repeatability of an observation in order to validate it and reach an unbiased conclusion.

Fieldwork is often the most valued, enjoyable, and memorable aspect of science courses. However, it also requires significant time for planning and execution. There are many aspects you should consider, including availability of portable scientific instruments, accessibility and limitations of the fieldwork site, weather conditions, and transportation and safety issues. State parks, geological trails, natural caves, nature preserves, and botanical gardens represent an excellent starting point for you to experiment with fieldwork trips if they apply to the goals of your course. They often have well-educated specialists who will help you plan and conduct the experience. They can also assist in guiding students to the most opportune locations for gathering their assigned observations and answering the many questions they may have.

Involving Students in Undergraduate Research. Encourage students to gain research experience in one of the laboratories in your college, university, or community. Such exposure to research has many advantages related to enhancing student learning. A research opportunity provides students with firsthand experience to understand how the information taught in the classroom originated. It will also increase their appreciation for the tremendous effort and skill involved in generating scientific knowledge and decrease their anxiety about learning science. Seeing real scientists at work and how they critically evaluate current literature, develop research ideas, interpret results, and interact with each other helps students develop logical thinking and problem-solving skills

These and other personal and professional skills, such as the careful organization and clear transmission of information, will become useful regardless of what type of careers individual students may choose. An undergraduate research experience will also help them decide if a research career is for them and which line of scholarly inquiry is most appealing. A stint in a research laboratory will undoubtedly enhance the admissions prospects of students who plan to apply to a high-caliber graduate or professional school. You will therefore be helping to prepare the next generation of scientists.

Assessment of Student Learning

As mentioned in other chapters in this book, your goal is not only to teach, but also to ascertain that students learn and, more important, comprehend new knowledge through your teaching. Try therefore to use different strategies to assess the extent and quality of their learning, both during lectures and in exams or labs throughout the course. Ask periodically during each lecture if anyone has questions or would like further clarification of presented information. At the end of each segment of your lecture, pose or present on the screen a multiple-choice question about a major concept to find out how many get it right. Use your instincts and watch for body language. Specifically, watch for signs of confusion, such as rolling eyes or head scratching.

Formal exams are also a valuable tool for assessing student learning. Exams in science courses come in many formats and differ in their depth and in how they target various levels of learning according to Bloom's taxonomy. Questions about constant parameters—for example, the speed of light or density of water—require only memorization skills and therefore serve to test for recall of individual pieces of information. Similarly, multiple-choice questions generally do not dig deep into higher levels of learning, unless you apply a modified format of this type of testing. For instance, ask students to justify their choice. More effective types of questions target the ability of students to comprehend scientific concepts and apply these concepts to new situations. Give them a problem to solve by utilizing different pieces of knowledge from the class. Labs, case presentations, and discussion of advanced reading material offer a good climate to test for comprehension and application of information. Writing term papers or open-book exam questions are also good ways to see if students can use this information to synthesize new concepts. More important, these formats better simulate what a student would do in the real world, where it is possible to consult different types of information sources in search of a solution to a problem.

Ultimately, science instructors bear a major responsibility in teaching the next generation about the foundation of various fields of science, and in keeping the students abreast of recent scientific developments. Striking the proper balance between these two types of information depends in large part on the educational level of the students and whether they are taking the course as a major, minor, or general requirement. But also pay attention to the goals of students in selecting a given science course. Some may select your course because of their future plans to become science teachers, researchers, or professionals who apply scientific knowledge at work. Others may elect to enroll simply because of their personal interest in the course topic. In general, you will probably find that most of your classes contain a wide variety of students, especially at the introductory level. Therefore you should strive to achieve a delivery strategy that is clear yet stimulating to all.

This can prove a daunting task. Do not be discouraged if you do not achieve it in your first few years of teaching. You will improve over time, provided that you are self-critical and self-reflective. Take detailed notes after each lecture or lab to review what worked well and what worked less well than you had hoped. Consult with more senior instructors or even attend some of their lectures. Perhaps you may decide to borrow various teaching techniques from others in formulating your own teaching style. In spite of the special challenges that science teachers face, their pivotal role in preparing the scientists, educators, engineers, and health professionals of tomorrow undoubtedly makes it all worthwhile.

8

Evaluating Your Teaching

Every teacher, however experienced, can benefit from an evaluation of his or her performance. Feedback from students or colleagues can alert you to aspects of your classroom behavior that might be distracting, irritating, or confusing to those you teach. Careful self-evaluation can also help you recognize weaknesses you might not have noticed if you had not made an effort to identify them.

Forms of Evaluation

In many, perhaps most, schools, you will have very little control over some forms of evaluation. Evaluations are often required by institutions—and sometimes even by law—and are one of the ways administrators monitor teachers. Such evaluations may become a permanent part of faculty personnel files and can have an impact on salaries and promotions. Some institutions require teachers to use standardized evaluation forms that may not be altered, although it is sometimes permissible to attach additional questions pertaining to a specific course. A formal evaluation typically comes at or near the end of a course.

But it is usually possible for teachers to utilize informal evaluations on their own, whatever the institution requires. (See Appendix F for examples.) To get informal feedback quickly, you might ask students to answer a question or two about some aspect of the class on note cards and return them to you at the end of class. A "spot" evaluation of that sort might ask students to tell you whether they understood the main points of a lecture or discussion; whether they found the required readings useful; or whether they saw the significance of a particular learning activity. For a broader assessment of your teaching, and of the course as a whole, you might construct a midterm evaluation, which could allow you to make changes before the end of the course.

Constructing Evaluations

If you do have any control over the form in which students are asked to evaluate your teaching, keep in mind some simple guidelines for constructing questions that will elicit useful responses. There are a number of different kinds of questions you can ask, each of which will elicit different kinds of responses. Some questions ask students to write out a response in their own words; others ask them to use a numerical scale to evaluate aspects of the course or the instructor. Evaluations often combine several types of questions.

If you are presenting your students with open-ended questions, be careful not to make them too broad. If you ask a single question such as "What do you think of this class?" you will likely get a range of responses that comment on everything from the assigned reading to the subject matter to your clothing choices. To avoid this problem, especially in evaluations used at the end of the term, ask students to assess specific parts of the course and specific aspects of your teaching abilities. For example, encourage appraisals of lecturing techniques, required reading, classroom atmosphere, availability of the instructor, use of multimedia material, or whatever other specific issues are relevant to your course.

It is usually best to have a mix of questions, some of which require written responses and some of which require ranking on a numbered scale. The former will give you a more textured response to your teaching, the latter a more statistically reliable one. Finally, arrange the questions into groups or clusters. One group of questions might ask students about your lectures, another about discussion sections or labs, another about assignments, another about collaborative exercises or independent projects.

Administering Evaluations

Written course evaluations demand rigorous administration if you want students to take them seriously. Explain to the students why you are doing an evaluation and how you will use the results. Make it clear that their evaluations will have no bearing on their grades in the course. Give them enough time to answer all of the questions and thank them for doing it. Keep all student evaluations anonymous and leave the room while the students are completing them. Ask volunteers to collect the evaluations, put them in an envelope, and deliver them to your department or mailbox or appropriate university office. If instructors collect the evaluations themselves, students will be rightly concerned that they might lose their anonymity.

Some schools require that evaluations conducted at the end of the course be sealed and not disclosed until the teacher has prepared and submitted final grades. Even if this is not a requirement, you should assure your students that you and your co-instructors will not read the evaluations until after the grades are done even if there is no rule requiring you to do so. Otherwise, students may be concerned that something they write will reveal their identity and affect your evaluation of their work.

Using Intermediaries for Evaluations

If you want a more probing evaluation, in which students are prodded to discuss your teaching in ways that a written form will not encourage them to do, you may wish to involve an intermediary. Students will naturally be reluctant to discuss with you directly their honest reactions to your teaching. You might consider arranging for them to have a conversation about your course with a neutral third party. If your institution employs teaching consultants (as some do), ask a consultant to come into your class for a few minutes toward the end of a period and interview your students after you have left. Discuss with the consultant in advance the questions you would like students to consider. If the class is small—for example, a seminar with ten to twelve students—such a discussion can take place with the entire group. Larger classes might break into smaller groups, discuss the questions among themselves, and then make group reports to the interviewer. The interviewer might take notes, summarize them for the class, ask for clarification, and then write up the results or discuss them with you. Alternatively, you might want the interviewer to give you the raw data of a classroom observation, rather than distilling it, if you fear an outsider might not properly interpret student reactions. While this method might take more class time than you are willing to give, it does provide a way for students to discuss their views without having to confront you directly.

If a consultant is not available, or if you prefer not to use one, another way to involve intermediaries in the evaluation process is to call on your own colleagues—fellow teachers who are themselves wrestling with many of the same problems and questions you are. The simplest way to get help from colleagues in the evaluation process is to solicit their comments on your syllabi, readings, and exams. A disinterested critic can often pick up on elements of your course materials—their tone, the overall impression they give—that might escape you. Such simple assessments often lead naturally to an exchange of ideas on teaching resources and techniques, which is often one of the most enjoyable parts of professional life.

Once you have established a relationship with some of your colleagues that makes peer evaluation comfortable for all of you, you might ask some of them to visit your classroom from time to time and offer advice. If you ask a peer to visit your class, give some thought to how to make it a productive assessment experience. Wait until you feel comfortable with the group of students before you ask an outsider to visit. The students will by then be focused less on the guest than on the class. Pick a typical classroom activity, rather than something unusual that you are trying for the first time. If possible, be sure there is student interaction or initiative rather than straight lecturing.

You will likely be somewhat nervous if a colleague is visiting your class. Try to reduce your anxiety by ensuring that you know exactly when the visitor is coming and by familiarizing your colleague with what the students are doing and how it fits into the larger aims of the course. If there are specific characteristics of your teaching on which you would like reactions or advice, alert your evaluator to them. And tell your students in advance that a visitor will sit in on a class. Do not surprise or confuse them by inserting a stranger into the room without notice.

Have a follow-up discussion with the evaluator as soon as possible after the visit rather than waiting until the class has faded from memory. If you want a written evaluation for your own records or your professional file, ask the visitor to compose one. You might also arrange for another visit later in the course to get an idea of how you are improving. Relationships among colleagues are different in every institution, and this kind of consultation may not seem appropriate in many cases. If you are an untenured member of a department, you may be reluctant to expose yourself to the scrutiny of more senior members, particularly if you do not know them very well. Even if there are no hierarchical issues, you may well feel uncomfortable interacting with your colleagues in this way—and you may have good reason to do so. But if you have a sufficiently secure and comfortable relationship with colleagues, it is often to your benefit to ask for their help.

Learning from Other Teachers

We all learn, to some extent, by imitation. Recall the teachers who most excited or inspired you. What was it about them that made their classes such memorable experiences? How did they spark your interest or push you to read the extra book or write the most difficult paper with success? Never discount your own experience on the other side of the desk as you try to figure out what makes a good class or great teacher.

When you think about courses you have taken yourself, consider particularly those most similar to the ones you are teaching now. What worked, and what didn't? Why? How was the class structured and conducted? Make a list of particularly useful assignments or reading materials. What lecture and discussion techniques were especially appealing? How were audiovisual materials employed? Were there any unusual teaching methods that were effective? Evaluate your own class experiences and use the information to benefit your teaching.

You need not rely solely on your memories of your own experience as a student. Your fellow teachers can also provide inspiration and examples. One of the best ways to evaluate your own teaching is to watch others teach and try to decide what you can learn from them. If possible, consider visiting the classes of fellow teachers, especially those you know and admire or whose reputations as teachers are good. If you are having trouble keeping your students awake during lectures, sit in on a class of a celebrated lecturer in your department. If discussions seem to end long before they should, visit a seminar with a reputation for being consistently lively.

The feasibility of visiting other instructors' classes (like the feasibility of having other teachers visit yours) will depend, of course, on the culture of your school or department—and your relationship with the teachers in question. Never attend another teacher's class without asking permission in advance, and only ask permission if you feel certain that the request will not seem intrusive or inappropriate. If you do ask to visit a colleague's class, make clear that it is because you are aware of his or her reputation as an excellent teacher and you think you might learn something from the experience.

If visiting classes is not possible or comfortable, you can learn a great deal from your colleagues simply through conversation—talking with them about how they teach, what assignments they use, and which techniques work for them and which don't. Everyone around you wrestles each day with the same problems you do, and one way or another you should make them into a resource for your own teaching.

You can learn from other teachers, but of course you cannot become them. When observing or talking with others, distinguish between techniques and approaches that you might find useful and those with which you would feel uncomfortable. Teaching is a very personal act, and what works for one instructor may not be compatible with the personality of another. But when you see a successful teaching technique that appears foreign to you, do not dismiss it too quickly. Experiment with different approaches; keep those that work for you and discard those that do not. Through trial and error and repeated practice in the classroom, you will define your own style. But shop around before you settle upon the teaching techniques most suited for you.

Remember that times—and students—change. What works now may not work at all in ten years, with a new generation of students. Some effective teaching methods are timeless, but others need to be adjusted as styles and customs change.

Assessing Yourself on Videotape

Some schools provide facilities that make it possible for you to videotape your classes and then review your performance, either on your own or with the help of teaching consultants. Even if your school does not provide such facilities, you can probably arrange to tape a class yourself with a simple home video camera. Instructors often find this a particularly valuable exercise, even if sometimes a difficult one.

Seeing yourself on camera in front of a class can be a humbling experience. Most of us have idealized views of what we look and sound like, and seeing ourselves as we appear to others can sometimes come as a shock. Few of us care to know how many times we say "uh" or "you know" in a fifty-minute period. But remember that what might look or sound strange to you is probably not at all strange to your students, who have always known you as you are now discovering yourself. Remember, too, that a videotape of a discussion or lecture is the "truest" representation of your teaching. In fact, in some ways it is less obtrusive than a visitor, particularly if the camera operates itself without a visiting technician. In a sense, it allows you to visit your own classroom. Once you get over the shock of seeing yourself through the camera's eye, there is much you can learn from the experience.

Some institutions have media services that can arrange for you to videotape your class. A campus teaching center, if you have one, can usually help you evaluate the results. It is often useful to watch the videotape with a trained evaluator, an experienced teacher, or a small group of colleagues. Whether you watch the tape by yourself or with others, evaluate it with specific written criteria, which might include interaction with students, organization, clarity of presentation, questioning techniques, classroom atmosphere, voice, and body movement.

As with other evaluations, tell the students ahead of time what will happen and pick a typical class. If you are handling the taping yourself, be sure the camera is at an angle that will permit a view of both you and your students. If possible, use two cameras, one focused on you and one on the students so that you can see what they are doing as you teach and how they are reacting to you. If you think taping is useful, try to tape more than one class during the term. Schedule a session in the fifth or sixth week of class so you will have enough time to evaluate the tape and act on suggestions for improvement, and then tape at least once more during the course to measure your progress. One advantage of videotape is that you can keep a record of your teaching to chart improvement.

Responding to Evaluations

It is a good idea to take advantage of some, perhaps many, of the various evaluation methods available to you. But you also need to use discretion in dealing with the results. As hard as it may be, try to separate the professional from the personal. Evaluations, from whatever source, are (or at least should be) responses to your professional abilities, not your personal qualities. Even if students make rude comments about your appearance or behavior or personality, keep in mind that the only basis for such comments is your performance in the classroom. The students know your teaching; they usually do not know you.

Try to remind yourself that you cannot be all things to all people. You will usually have some students who do not like the way you teach or the subject matter you present but find themselves in your course anyway. The larger the course, the more malcontents you are likely to encounter. Many instructors are tempted to ignore the positive evaluations of their performance, even if such evaluations are the vast majority of the total, and remember only the critical comments. If several students in a large lecture class say your lectures are dull while most of the others find them lively, look at the numbers. On the other hand, don't ignore criticisms that crop up repeatedly in evaluations. Look for recurring comments in student evaluations rather than the isolated reaction. One glowing response in a set of mediocre reactions should not leave you satisfied any more than one negative evaluation in the midst of positive ones should leave you distressed.

If evaluations come in the middle of the term, separate the criticisms into various categories. Look for ones that you can act on immediately. Identify those that you might consider using as the basis of change in future courses. On some points, you might let the students know that you are modifying classroom activities or your teaching style as a result of suggestions they made that you found helpful. That can give them a stronger sense of participation in the learning process, of being to some degree partners in your common effort. But there will likely be some aspects of your course that you will decide not to change regardless of criticism.

Identify problems with which you need outside help. If you're having a chronic problem that defies solution, with a class, an individual student, or any aspect of teaching, seek assistance—from a colleague, from a teaching center, from friends or family members who may know you well enough to have suggestions that would not occur to professional associates. Articulating your frustrations often helps you to clarify the problems, get constructive feedback, and collaborate on ways to improve your situation. It also helps to talk it out and realize that you are not the only instructor who has faced difficulties.

Realize that you can be both a good scholar and a good teacher. The two are not mutually exclusive. Being a good teacher does not mean that you are not a "real scholar." Great research scholars are often effective instructors. A truly successful academic life draws strength from both teaching and research, which are often complementary.

Finding Campus Teaching Resources

There are usually many resources in schools, colleges, and universities that can help improve your teaching, some of which may not appear immediately useful for that purpose. The obvious place to start for any beginning instructor is in your own department, which can give you information about teaching conventions and traditions in your field. Your department might also provide sample syllabi, equipment, a specialized library, an audiovisual collection, and, of course, the expertise of its members. See if your department sponsors teaching workshops or an evaluation program.

Many campuses have teaching centers specifically intended for new instructors. Staffed by professionals who offer a range of support activities, they often conduct ongoing teaching workshops, provide individual counseling, assist in creating evaluations, review videotapes of classes, and offer a library on teaching.

If you are a graduate student teacher, consult your department's or institution's graduate student organizations, which can be another valuable source for teaching handbooks, evaluations, workshops, and general information about teaching at a college or university. Because such organizations are usually staffed and run by graduate students, they have the advantage of giving you the view from the trenches rather than the headquarters.

While we don't usually think of the library as a place to improve our teaching, reference librarians trained in specific subject areas are an essential resource for anyone teaching a class with research as a component. They will familiarize you with collections, help to plan research assignments, and, most important, give specialized library tours. Some college libraries even offer term-paper services for both students and teachers. With advance warning of your research assignments, librarians can guide you and your students to resources you may not have known existed.

Student learning centers are designed to help students more than teachers. But because they tend to focus on study skills and writing deficiencies, they are in a good position to give you advice about structuring assignments. They are also places to which you can refer students who are having difficulties with the work in your class. If you have students with learning disabilities in your class, your institution likely has a support service that can arrange for note takers, signers, and alternative exam administration (for example, exams without time limits, oral exams, or exams taken by computer).

Campus media or audiovisual centers may be able to help you arrange videotaping and provide equipment for classroom use. Some maintain a lending library of videos, films, slides, and audiotapes. They may also teach you how to use the equipment or provide you with someone who can operate it for you.

A campus computer center is an obvious place to learn how to integrate online activities into your course or how to supplement classroom activities. It might also provide you with software to use in your teaching. Some centers offer courses on using computers for teaching.

The Internet can supply all sorts of teaching resources, including sample syllabi, departments' and professors' Web pages, teaching centers at other institutions, publishing houses, bibliographies, government education initiatives at all levels, and many more. Many professional associations now identify useful and appropriate Web sites. Keep an eye out, too, for articles on teaching in professional newsletters, in the *Chronicle of Higher Education,* and in other publications which try to share teaching experiences broadly.

Self-evaluation is an ongoing process in every teacher's career, from the graduate student teaching a first class to the instructor with thirty years' experience. Good teaching requires constant reflection on your preparation, your techniques, and your students' needs and interests. This may seem like an onerous task, but in fact it will refresh and recharge what you do in the classroom, with positive results for everyone involved in the learning process.

Teaching as a Part-Time Instructor

Many graduate students and other new teachers have their first classroom experiences as part-time instructors. Graduate students may serve as readers, graders, or leaders of discussion sections in a lecture course. They may also teach undergraduate seminars, advise research projects, and give prepared lectures in their own sections or as part of a survey course. Part-time adjunct faculty, sometimes called "contingent faculty," generally teach their own courses, but usually at a lower salary than their tenure-track counterparts and with little or no employee benefits. Undergraduate education today, for better or worse, relies increasingly on graduate student and adjunct teaching. Part-time instructors face the normal issues and demands that all teachers do, but they also face special problems, whether they are graduate student teaching assistants or adjuncts.

As teaching assistants, graduate students gain classroom experience important to their future professional careers as teachers and scholars. But being a successful instructor at the same time as being a successful graduate student takes careful planning. Students need to balance their limited time between teaching duties and dissertation work. Building constructive relationships with professors and learning how to deal with students in and out of the classroom are also important. Finally, you should use your teaching experiences in graduate school to help develop skills that will help you when you enter the job market.

Adjunct instructors face many of the same challenges as any other teacher, but they usually have no guarantee of continued employment. Many adjuncts teach at several different institutions at the same time and must adjust to different working conditions and campus policies as they move between institutions. Adjuncts are usually less involved in the campus community than full-time faculty, sometimes by choice but often due to university policies. The unhappy result is a lack of collegiality with their tenure-track counterparts and a sense of marginality, at least in professional terms.

Graduate Students

GUARDING YOUR TIME

Pursuing graduate education and teaching classes simultaneously is a constant juggling act. Good teaching, particularly at the beginning, can take as much or more time than your graduate studies. Keeping the two careers in balance is not always easy. The main purpose of being in graduate school is to receive an education and build the foundation of a professional career. Teaching may be an integral part of that career, but it may not be the primary reason you sought a doctorate. It is certainly not the only thing, or even the most important thing, in determining your professional future. So while you strive to be a good teacher, don't lose sight of the path to your degree.

That is not always an easy thing to do. Teaching will consume as much time and energy as you let it, particularly if you enjoy it. Budget your teaching time carefully so it does not intrude too heavily on your own work. The more organized your work schedule is, the less stressful your graduate experience will be, although some strain is inevitable. Set aside particular days or parts of days in which you prepare for the classes you teach and leave other times for your own coursework or dissertation research. Then follow the routine. Schedule office hours for the days when your classes meet so you will not have to spend more time than necessary on campus. Obviously, you cannot plan for every contingency, and your schedule may go awry due to unexpected events. But if you ration your time with care and conviction, you will experience more satisfaction and make better progress on both your teaching and research.

Remember also to relax. Getting away from both teaching and research is essential for your mental well-being. Try to take at least a day and a night off every week. Socialize with friends or family. Spending all of your time preparing for the next class or searching for the ultimate source may cause you to resent your work—and lose energy and enthusiasm for it. Contrary to what some may believe or claim, you can become a good teacher, student, and scholar without sacrificing your personal life.

RELATIONSHIPS WITH PROFESSORS

The most common way for graduate students to begin their teaching careers is by leading small discussion sections for a large lecture course. As a teaching assistant (TA), your role is set by the professor, who may or may not give you the kind of guidance you expect and need. Some professors are active supervisors of their teaching assistants. They hold weekly meetings to coordinate section activities, and they get regular input from their TAs about all aspects of the course. Others give you the syllabus, expect you to come to lectures, and leave everything else to you. Still others hover between these two approaches. Whatever the situation you encounter, you will, of course, want to get as much as you can out of your teaching experience, do as well as you can for your students, and maintain a professional relationship with the professor in charge—all at the same time.

Remember that as a teaching assistant, you are in charge of your section but not of the course as a whole. No matter how much you may dislike a required reading or a paper topic or lecture content, it is still your responsibility to teach it carefully and explain clearly why the assignment or the material is important. Many professors will ask their TAs for advice, and at that point it is appropriate to offer your observations about some of the drawbacks and strengths of various aspects of the course. But on the whole, you must live with the professor's decisions about the structure of the course and try to make the best of them.

When you begin a new teaching assignment, clarify your duties and responsibilities with the professor. What are his or her goals for the discussion sections? What are his or her expectations for TAs? Are you expected to attend every class, even if you have heard the lectures previously? Are you expected to grade all the papers? Give reading quizzes regularly? Hold extra review sessions before exams? While most professors explain the various parts of the job to TAs before the start of the term, some may assume you will know what you are supposed to do. To avoid problems later, ask early about general expectations and specific duties. The danger is that you may have find yourself doing more than you had anticipated, but at least you will have the benefit of advance knowledge.

If possible, meet regularly with the professor to discuss the progress of the course. If the professor holds weekly meetings with his TAs, use them to clarify subject matter, exchange teaching ideas, and resolve classroom problems that may have arisen. If the professor does not hold regular meetings, you might suggest that he or she do so. With the professor's permission, you might even try to organize the TAs into their own group to discuss teaching every week or so. If necessary, try to find some other occasion—office hours, before or after class—to ask the professor for help and guidance when appropriate.

Because TAs seldom have the luxury of choosing for whom they will work, clashes of personality or differences of opinion over matters such as teaching methodology or grading standards are not uncommon. Most instructors are eager to make your teaching experience rewarding and enjoyable. But you may find yourself assisting a professor with whom you have had an unpleasant experience as a graduate student or with whom you experience disagreements and conflicts. Often you will have no choice but to act like a professional and do your best. But if the conflict threatens to affect your teaching, speak directly to the professor. As awkward and difficult as such a conversation might be, it is almost always better to clear the air rather than let your frustration and anger build—and possibly infect your relations with your students. If problems persist, talk to your adviser, the department's faculty member in charge of TAs (if there is one), or the department chair. If problems are particularly serious, you might wish to seek outside help, perhaps from graduate student organizations or the campus teaching center. Often the professor in charge of the course is also important to your future in other ways. It is important, therefore, to manage your relationship with him or her carefully, especially given the imbalance of power between you.

RELATIONSHIPS WITH STUDENTS

Graduate student instructors also face special challenges in their relationships with their students because the instructors are in an unusual position in the professional hierarchy of the university. If you are a graduate teaching assistant, you are not just a teacher to your students; you are also their intermediary with the professor. If you teach your own class, you take on the role of a professor, but without the status of a regular faculty member. Your students may or may not be aware of your position within the university, but you certainly are. And you will be rightly concerned about conducting yourself in a way that will meet with the approval of your faculty supervisors while also meeting the needs of your students. Whatever position you occupy, you need to conduct yourself in a professional manner with your colleagues and, most importantly, your students. Striving for a friendly yet professional relationship with them is a crucial part of teaching.

Whether you are a teaching assistant or an instructor in charge of your own course, your position gives you a certain amount of power and authority in and out of the classroom. No matter how friendly you are with your students, you should not forget that your relationship is not one of absolute or even relative equality. Be friendly toward your students, but maintain a professional distance from them. Although you may be only a few years older than they are, it is your job to demonstrate a sincere interest in their education and encourage them to develop a strong commitment to intellectual life.

Insist on mutual respect in the classroom—both in your relationship with your students and in their relationships with one another. Treat your students with fairness and respect. Do not intimidate them with intellectual or disciplinary authority. Intervene quickly when students are behaving inappropriately toward each other. Welcome them during office hours and listen to their academic concerns. Treat them all equally, without favoritism.

Create an atmosphere of tolerance in your classroom. In many different disciplines, particularly social science and humanities, it is common to discuss sensitive topics, among them issues of race, ethnicity, gender, sexuality, politics, and religion. Encourage respect for alternative viewpoints through listening, questioning, and reasoned argument. No doubt most of your students will have strong opinions, but remind them that convincing opinions—and good scholarship—stem from sound logic and reliable evidence. Try to use such discussions to further students' understanding of the process of scholarly inquiry.

Clarify your expectations and rules early in the term. Students want to know what you expect of them in the course and in the classroom. The course requirements are listed on the syllabus. What you will need to establish during the first few meetings are the tone and atmosphere of your own class. How much structure will you build into discussions? Does a student need to raise her hand if she wants to make a comment? Will you tolerate late arrivals and early departures? Will you allow students to eat in class or text their friends?

RESOLVING DISPUTES WITH STUDENTS

Disputes with students over such issues as grades, behavior, academic honesty, or individual personality are common parts of the teaching experience. In general, it is best to confront such problems rather than hope they will go away by themselves, especially since you will probably meet with your students regularly during the term.

If you have a personal disagreement with a student, talk to him or her about it in private before it gets worse. Try to arrange a solution that clears the air and will not inhibit the student's learning or your teaching. Remember that it is unlikely that you will please all the students all the time. Do not interpret this as a personal failure. You do want your students to enjoy coming to class and even to like you. But you cannot compromise your responsibilities to the course, to your students, and to yourself to achieve that goal.

If a student is rude or obstreperous to other students, speak to him or her the first time it happens. It is probably best to acknowledge such behavior in class simply by cutting the student off, ideally in a way that will not embarrass the offender. If the behavior recurs, speak to the student after class and explain calmly but firmly why you find the behavior unacceptable. In any case, do not let it go unnoticed because it may become worse. But try to avoid a confrontation during class—it may escalate unnecessarily because neither you nor the student wishes to "lose face" in front of the others.

A more common problem is complaints about grades. Students will be aware that you, not the professor, are grading their work. They may also be aware of the grade scale that other teaching assistants in the same course are using. It is tempting to look scornfully at students who protest their grades. But you should recall that students are under tremendous pressure to maintain high grade point averages to position themselves well for jobs or graduate schools. And you should also keep in mind that sometimes their complaints are justified. Therefore it is important to take grade grievances seriously. You can preempt some problems by clearly explaining your criteria for evaluating specific papers, assignments, and exams in advance. But no amount of forethought will eliminate all complaints. So give the student a fair hearing. Then explain clearly and with specific examples why he or she earned that particular grade. Whether or not you reread the paper or exam and revise the grade depends on the policy you or the professor has set for the course as a whole. In any event, remain consistent when further grievances arise. If the student remains unsatisfied, suggest that he or she take the paper or exam to the professor in charge of the course (providing that the professor is willing to consider such complaints). Do not feel that a student who challenges your grade is undermining your authority. The professor is the ultimate authority, and it is reasonable for students to expect a final hearing from him or her.

PLAGIARISM AND CHEATING

If you encounter plagiarism, which is far from unusual, you will need to think not just about the student, but about yourself. Do you have the authority to deal with the issue on your own? If you are a TA in a course taught by a professor, you should bring any such problems to the professor's attention. If he or she asks you to handle it, then you should do so in the same way an instructor of any rank would proceed (see chapter 5). But be sure you have the authority to act before you become embroiled in what will likely be a very unpleasant and difficult dispute. A graduate student is not usually in a very strong position to deal with so explosive a problem. If someone else—a professor, a committee, an administrator—can handle the problem for you, it is usually best to let them do so.

The same principles apply to suspected cheating on examinations. Consult with your professor or department about how they handle such matters. Pass on responsibility for handling it if you can. But do not permit cheating to continue without a response, and if necessary take steps on your own to deal with it.

If the decision about how to deal with plagiarism or cheating is yours alone, you have a number of options. These include giving the student a chance to redo the work, failing him on the work in question, or giving her an "F" for the course as a whole. If you or your professor has set a clear policy at the beginning of the term, stick to it. If you have not, evaluate the seriousness of the problem and the motives of the student before deciding how to respond. Before taking action be sure to listen to the student's point of view. And be prepared for an emotional response that may run the gamut from indignation and denial to tears and remorse.

ETHICAL DILEMMAS

Sometimes your dual role as teacher and student may leave you with a sense of divided loyalties, uncertain about where your professional responsibilities lie. The position of teaching assistant can become even stickier since the students think of you as the buffer between them and the professor. Students may see you as a personal confidant rather than as a teacher. You may be tempted to consider some members of your classes to be friends as much as students. It is important, therefore, to establish ground rules for your relationships with students to avoid the possibility of awkwardness, embarrassment, or worse.

Maintain a professional distance from your students. Listen to their academic concerns but do not try to become their psychoanalyst or their parent. You are unlikely to be qualified to help students with serious psychological or personal problems—and you may cause more harm than good if you try. If students have such problems, refer them to the appropriate professional resources on or off campus.

Never become romantically involved with a student. The line between friendly and inappropriate behavior is thin and gray, so do not cross or even approach it. Schools and universities usually have strict policies about what constitutes an improper relationship or sexual harassment, and such rules may include behavior that falls far short of the legal definition. Follow them rigorously and scrupulously, even if they seem excessively strict. After the course has concluded, avoid becoming personally involved with any of your former students for a significant period of time to avoid creating a perception of impropriety within your institution that could harm you or the student.

If your institution has no guidelines regarding improper relationships—which is unlikely—use common sense. Avoid meeting students alone in your home or theirs. Avoid unusual physical contact. And avoid comments or language that others might interpret as flirtatious or provocative. It is usually unwise, for example, to comment on a student's clothes or hairstyle. In today's world, many are sensitive about matters of sexuality and intimacy, and whether or not you believe such sensitivities are justified you must be aware of them and be careful not to offend them. You can pay a heavy price for failing to do so.

Always conduct yourself in a professional manner with fellow graduate students and faculty as well. Making a personal criticism of a professor or another TA to your students, your fellow TAs, or other faculty members is unprofessional. Always keep the confidences of faculty, fellow TAs, and most of all your students. Above all, keep grades confidential. Never discuss student grades or other personal information with students, TAs, or faculty other than the professor in charge of your course.

Respond seriously to student complaints about professors. Obviously, this calls for tact and timing, and for an evaluation of the character of the professor involved and your relationship with him or her. But if students have complaints that you think are justified, it is usually a good idea to relay them to the professor—making clear that the suggestions are coming from students, and that your goal is to be helpful. If you meet regularly with the professor along with other TAs, such a meeting may be a good time to bring up problems that students have mentioned. That way, you can create a discussion of it among colleagues rather than a possible confrontation with a professor. You alone, however, must decide whether the consequences to you of bringing a complaint to a professor's attention are likely to outweigh the value of airing grievances. Here, as in many other cases, you must balance your own stake in your relationship with a professor against what you think your responsibilities to your students are.

Avoid departmental politics. Every department, no matter how cooperative and collegial, has internal controversies that divide the faculty and may create problems for graduate students. Some, like the issue of graduate student unionization in some universities, could affect you directly. Others, such as hiring decisions, may have only a peripheral impact. In either case, remember that your main purpose in graduate school is to get an education. If you do get involved in a controversial issue, try to do it in a professional way. Always strive to remain calm and conciliatory. As a graduate student, you are in a vulnerable position, and direct confrontations with faculty can threaten your future. Unless you believe your personal or academic integrity is at stake, it is generally best to avoid such confrontations.

TEACHING AND CAREER PLACEMENT

Once you are near the end of your graduate education and the job market looms on the horizon, the place of teaching in your professional training takes on a new dimension. In the tight market most graduate students face today, potential employers have become more demanding of their candidates. Except at the most elite research universities (and not invariably there either), scholarly credentials—your dissertation and other written work—are usually not sufficient. In liberal arts colleges, state universities, and community colleges, where most of the jobs are, teaching is often more important than research. Prospective employers may thus have more interest in your potential as a teacher than in your performance as a scholar. It is not uncommon for both universities and colleges to ask a candidate to teach a class as part of the campus interview. Give careful thought, therefore, to how you can use your teaching experience to give you an edge in the job market.

The most obvious way to prepare for the job market is to prepare a teaching dossier. Be sure that at least one of your references addresses your ability in the classroom. Such a reference should come from someone with whom, or for whom, you have taught. Ideally, it should come from someone who has observed you in the classroom and with whom you have discussed teaching techniques and course planning. If you have been a TA, ask your supervising professor.

Think seriously about how you will discuss teaching in a job interview. Interviewers will almost certainly address teaching, even in a preliminary interview held at a professional meeting. Be prepared to outline some of the following to potential employers:

- kinds of classes you have already taught, those you feel capable of teaching, and those you would particularly like to teach (you may even wish to develop syllabi for them)
- types of techniques you have developed that might suggest your talents in the classroom
- kinds of assignments you have designed for students—the more creative the better, at least in some instances
- plans for how you would teach graduate courses (if you are interviewing for a position in a university with a graduate program)

- books you would use in particular courses (bear in mind the identity of the interviewers)
- ways you might incorporate your own research into your teaching

Many graduate students keep a formal record of their teaching career to use in the job search. Consider creating a portfolio as soon as you start teaching and adding to it as you progress in your career. A portfolio should include syllabi from courses in which you have taught (and any hypothetical syllabi you may have prepared for courses you would like to teach). It should also include examples of different types of assignments you have given students, particularly successful ones, along with an explanation of the rationale behind the assignments. Your portfolio might also include the results of student evaluations of your teaching, if they have been statistically compiled in a form available to you, or even a sample of the actual evaluation forms, which your department may keep on file. Include as well a short statement describing your teaching techniques, philosophy, or goals. If available, you might even include a DVD of you in the classroom.

If you do decide to create a teaching portfolio, it will, of course, reflect your own experiences and interests and may not include precisely the items suggested here. Whatever kind of portfolio you create, try to make it flexible. Since different potential employers will have different teaching needs, tailor your credentials to the particular characteristics of the job. There is nothing dishonest about this practice as long as the credentials are accurately presented. An elite research university might expect evidence of different kinds of teaching talents than would a small college, for example, and it is perfectly appropriate to present yourself in the most suitable light for each circumstance.

Teaching portfolios are not an ordinary part of many applications. So you should not send one to potential employers unsolicited—just as you normally would not send chapters of your dissertation until requested to do so. Mention it in your application letter as one of the things you will send on request. If you are invited later to a campus interview, take the portfolio with you (if you have not previously submitted it) and look for an appropriate moment to share it.

Contingent Faculty

PROFESSIONAL RESPONSIBILITIES

In 2005, the U.S. Department of Education reported that part-time faculty represented approximately 46 percent of all faculty in institutions of higher learning, an increase from 30 percent in 1975. Whether at community colleges, four-year private institutions, or state universities, part-time faculty are one of the fastest growing segments of higher education. As such, they bring special issues to the teaching and learning table. One of the most important concerns is that of the adjunct faculty's responsibilities to his or her students, and the educational institution's and academic department's responsibilities to the adjunct. Because contingent faculty usually receive lower salaries than their tenure-track, full-time counterparts, and are often on the fringe of departmental and institutional professional culture, these questions are even more difficult to negotiate. As an adjunct hired for a specific purpose, you have the right to know the terms and conditions of your employment as well as the specific expectations your employers have of you. Conversely, the institution and department have the right to know what they can expect from you in terms of professional responsibilities and commitment.

Most part-time faculty offer their own courses according to the arrangement made at the time of their employment. But such arrangements often run the gamut from specific conditions contractually defined to vague commitments finalized verbally. It is best to obtain from the institution a written agreement that specifies the courses you will teach in the time period of your employment in addition to specific salary and employee benefits. Are there any other professional duties that the university or college expects of you? For example, are you supposed to hold regular office hours, attend department faculty meetings, or participate in a student orientation program? If you develop an online course, do you or the university own the intellectual rights to it?

Before the term or semester begins, make an appointment with the department chair to discuss his or her expectations of your professional duties. This is the time to ask questions and gather as much information as possible that will help you plan your courses. What may seem obvious to the department chair may not be to you. For whom is the course intended, and what is its place in the department's curriculum? Do you have the freedom to order your own books, or is there a shared text (which is sometimes the case for introductory courses)? How many students are usually in the course? Is there any type of assignment that is expected and with what frequency? Introductory and advanced courses sometimes have reading, writing, project, or laboratory requirements determined by the department's faculty. If there is more than one section of the course being taught, are instructors expected to coordinate assignments or exams? Is an exam required, and, if so, what is the expected format (essay, multiple choice, etc.)? Be sure that you have the answers to all of these questions before you plan your syllabus. It is critical that you understand in advance the department's academic culture and requirements so that you can match your teaching style to the students' expectations.

Another important issue is supervision and evaluation of your classroom teaching. Most universities require part-time faculty to administer a student evaluation at the end of a course, but some also ask for peer evaluations by the department's full-time faculty and/or the chair, to be completed by a certain date. Be sure that you understand the university requirements for peer classroom observations and performance reviews, particularly if there is a written component that follows the evaluation. Then ascertain the formal procedures and time frame you must follow if you wish to contest the evaluator's conclusions regarding your teaching.

Prior to the start of the term is also the time to find out the availability of university and department resources for adjunct faculty. Will you have an office, and if so, is it shared? Do you have access to a telephone and a computer with an Internet connection? What are the university procedures to obtain an e-mail account? What are departmental policies on photocopying materials? Can you get secretarial assistance if necessary? Although universities should provide all faculty with such resources, as a part-time instructor you cannot and should not assume that all will be readily available to you. Ask first to avoid misunderstandings later.

Finally, acquaint yourself with the teaching resources offered by the university and department. As a part-time instructor, do you have access to the same campus resources offered to tenure-track faculty? Many campuses offer instructional assistance that will range from formal workshops requiring enrollment and attendance on a regular basis to more casual "brown-bag lunches" that provide faculty the opportunity for cross-disciplinary discussions on teaching. In addition, larger universities often have offices designed specifically to assist faculty in improving undergraduate instruction and technology training. Find out what is available and how you can take advantage of it. Even if you are only teaching one course for one semester, there is still an opportunity to benefit from your temporary professional environment.

TIME COMMITMENT

Like graduate students whose primary responsibility is to their research agenda, part-time instructors usually have other professional demands on their time for a variety of reasons. Some contingent faculty hold "day jobs" and teach a course or two for personal interest; others who have been unable to secure a tenure-track position are part-time out of financial necessity, sometimes juggling several adjunct positions at different institutions simultaneously. Still others have a working spouse and choose to teach part-time for personal or family reasons. Whatever your situation is, like any professional, you will have to deal with varying demands on your time. Teaching can easily consume an extraordinary amount of your time, especially if you allow it and enjoy it. You will therefore need to prioritize your responsibilities, particularly if you're seeking full-time employment while working as an adjunct.

Preparing your courses, holding office hours, and grading student assignments are usually your primary responsibilities as a part-time instructor, unless otherwise specified in your employment agreement. While you should give the time and energy necessary for teaching an intellectually stimulating course for both you and your students, and meeting the university's expectations, you also need to think carefully about the extent of your commitment to the institution. Teaching one course during a single semester without the promise of continued employment should not take all of your attention to the exclusion of other responsibilities. If, on the other hand, the part-time position may become a tenure-track job for which you might apply, then you may want to commit more time beyond what the department reasonably and typically requires of adjuncts. Think carefully about how your part-time position fits into your current and future personal and professional plans.

CLASSROOM ISSUES

As part-time faculty, you will likely encounter the same array of class-room issues faced by tenure-track faculty, ranging from plagiarism to motivating students to disciplinary problems. What makes your position unlike that of your tenure-track colleagues, however, is your contingent status. The way your institution and department treats part-time faculty may affect the way you confront academic and disciplinary issues that emerge during the daily routine of instruction and the administration of a course. It is, therefore, important to know the extent of support you can expect if a problem arises in your classroom.

Grade complaints, plagiarism, cheating, sexual harassment, and class-room disciplinary issues are no different for contingent faculty than for regular faculty. Be sure that you are familiar with departmental and university regulations regarding all of these. Before you begin teaching, have a frank conversation with your department chair about university policies and the procedures to follow if you find yourself in any of these situations with students. If the campus faculty is unionized, you may also want to find out if the union provides part-time faculty with protection, and if so, what its services are.

A particularly thorny issue that may affect contingent faculty is academic freedom. By definition, most contingent faculty do not have job security from year to year or even semester to semester. Because student evaluations may determine who is rehired and who is not, part-time faculty may be reticent about trying innovative teaching methods that depart from the norm of the department. Or they might avoid controversial issues so as not to alienate any of their students. The essence of the classroom is a free and civil exchange of academic ideas without fear of censorship or retribution from the university administration, but contingent faculty do not always enjoy this privilege. The best you can do is to be as professional as possible with your students, your instruction, and your courses.

FINDING A PROFESSIONAL COMMUNITY

It is often difficult for part-time faculty to see themselves as an integral part of an academic department and the larger campus community. Their contingent status means that they are not on campus on a regular basis, and they often do not participate in shared governance through committee work. Often they do not attend department meetings. This may leave you thinking that you are the casual labor of the department, teaching your courses for less salary without any real prospects of permanent employment. This may be acceptable for those who choose part-time work because of personal circumstances, but it can leave other adjuncts who are seeking a tenure-track position feeling underappreciated and demoralized. To avoid this outcome, make the most of your temporary academic position to gain benefits that may help you land a full-time job.

Think about how you can use your teaching position to your advantage. If you are offering a course not directly related to your field of expertise, see it as an opportunity to broaden your academic knowledge and teaching repertoire. The same is also true for the types of courses you may teach. Does this adjunct position give you the opportunity to teach large lectures and smaller seminars, or work with teaching assistants, or experiment with different types of teaching methods, perhaps integrating technology on a regular basis? Do you teach a wide variety of students in terms of their academic abilities and interests? All of these can only add to your teaching experience, making you a more versatile and desirable job candidate to potential employers. Remember that your goal is to make your teaching an asset as you build your professional resume.

Likewise, participating in department and campus activities and committees can also work to your advantage. If your time and college policies allow, volunteer to serve on department and university committees. At the very least, regularly attend department meetings if possible. Partake in activities that will have an impact on your teaching and your students. For example, attend instructional workshops or review teaching materials used in common for courses taught by all department faculty. By doing so, you will become a more integral member of the campus community. And you will gain expertise and experience for your professional future, whether it lies at this or some other institution.

Finally, acquaint yourself with the various organizations, Web sites, and academic journals designed specifically for adjunct faculty. As the overall number of contingent faculty has grown during the last ten years, so have the resources that address issues unique to part-time instructors. Professional organizations such as the American Association of University Professors, American Federation of Teachers, and the National

Education Association address the needs of adjuncts by outlining a set of "best practices" for employment procedures, compensation, working conditions, and rehiring. The professional organization serving your particular discipline may also have a committee focusing on adjunct issues. The Organization of American Historians (OAH), for example, has a Committee on Part-Time and Adjunct Employment that serves as an advocate and sounding board for issues affecting adjuncts in the history profession. (In 2003, both the OAH and American Historical Association issued a joint statement on the use of adjuncts and part-time faculty in the historical profession.) See also the American Chemical Society's "Guide to Classroom Instruction for Adjunct Faculty," the American Studies Association's "Statement on Standards in Graduate Education," and the Modern Language Association's "Statement on the Use of Part-Time and Full-Time Adjunct Faculty."

For more general assistance, consult the Coalition on the Academic Workforce (http://www.academicworkforce.org/). Founded by a variety of professional organizations in the humanities and social sciences, it is another advocacy group that works on behalf of contingent faculty. Its Web site offers policy statements and practical resources for part-time faculty. Composed of volunteer activists and operating at the grassroots level, the Coalition of Contingent Academic Labor (http://www.aaup.org/AAUP/issues/contingent/cocal.htm) maintains a Web site and organizes a biennial international conference to address ongoing issues affecting contingent faculty. The journal *Adjunct Advocate* and its Web site, Adjunctnation.com, also offer a wide variety of resources for contingent faculty including a listserv, information about grants and job openings, sample syllabi, a bibliography of professional books, and practical classroom teaching suggestions.

Teaching as a graduate student or an adjunct instructor is often extraordinarily rewarding—and a great deal of fun. It can also be difficult and demanding. Whatever the experience, try to act professionally, serve your students well, and draw from your teaching whatever personal lessons (and professional benefits) you can for the future. Ideally, they will sustain you during the awkward moments that you will inevitably encounter and that pose challenges to every teacher at every level and every stage of his or her career.

Creating and Sustaining an Inclusive Classroom

A key goal of education today is to prepare students to participate successfully in our increasingly diverse and global society. The demographics of college and university student bodies have changed dramatically in recent years. The enrollment of women has almost doubled since the 1960s. Currently, women outnumber men as degree recipients at every level except the doctorate. African American students have grown from 5 percent of the freshman class in the 1960s to more than 11 percent today. Today, Latino students make up approximately 7 percent of the entering class, and Asian American students about 8 percent. Education demographers project that Latino and Asian and Pacific Islander communities will continue to grow more than any other groups. And most colleges are becoming increasingly international. American institutions continue to enroll nearly a quarter of all international students worldwide. In contrast to this quickly diversifying student population, approximately 80 percent of teachers are white.

Diversity means more than differences in race and ethnicity. Students arrive on campus with a broad range of social experiences, learning-related needs, and aspirations. The presence of lesbian, gay, bisexual, and transgender (LGBT) students is increasingly visible at every level of education. American schools host more international students than ever before. Students come to campus with earlier diagnoses of learning disabilities, and we see a steady increase in students with a broad range of psychosocial needs such as drug and alcohol recovery issues, eating disorders, or depression.

Inclusive classrooms are an essential component of students' preparation for professional, civic, and interpersonal success. Our students are changing, and we should, too. Multiculturally inclusive teaching is a commitment to address the variety of the ways students may feel included or excluded in the college classroom.

The goal of this chapter is not to make you a diversity expert. It does offer general guidelines to help you better design, teach, and assess courses that address the learning needs of an increasingly diverse undergraduate population.

General Practices of Multicultural Course Design

Early work on multicultural teaching focused on additional content to address issues of gender, race, and ethnicity. This reflected the scholarship of fields that were new at the time such as ethnic, women's, and lesbian and gay studies. Today, multiculturalism also includes teacher self-reflection, pedagogical innovation, and understanding who students are and what they bring to the classroom.

UNIVERSAL DESIGN

Universal design practices allow you to clarify assignments, detail expectations, specify deadlines, and offer examples for performance. Breaking large or complicated assignments down into components helps students build toward the final goal. In this structure, students receive incremental developmental feedback on smaller pieces, rather than relying only on a final submission that becomes "sink or swim." Writing assignments are well suited to this design. Feedback on early drafts benefits students for whom English is a second language, such as international students or first-generation immigrants, by reducing their anxiety, focusing efforts, and building skills.

Another aspect of universal design is to offer students multiple options for expressing mastery of the material. Of course, all options must align with the learning outcome goals for the course, be equal in terms of expectations, and rigor. An example of multiple expressions of the same assignment might be a choice between writing a paper, giving an in-class presentation, or creating a digital story based on an interview. International students may have higher confidence in their writing skills than their speaking skills. Therefore, they may prefer an option of writing a paper to giving an oral presentation.

To incorporate more universal design principles, experiment with a variety of instructional methods. In addition to lecturing, encourage students to learn about how to work together by including peer-learning activities early on. Consider assigning students to diverse groups when you want to encourage them to get to know each other well enough to learn from each other's experiences. Group assignments offer students the benefit of a diverse range of perspectives, more complex analyses, and experience with collaborative problem-solving efforts. A different venue for these efforts are online options, where students can work together or at their own pace, continue or start discussions, and ask questions about homework assignments.

In addition to the general principles just described, consider explicitly articulating your course-related diversity goals. Such goals include cultivating a respect for diverse perspectives; developing an ability and willingness to work effectively in diverse groups; being sensitive to gender, class, or race differences. More broadly, you might expect students to identify and reject narrow/oppositional thinking that reduces issues to only two sides (right/wrong, us/them) or engage in intergroup dialogues. By making such learning outcomes explicit, you also make clear your broad commitment to fairness and equity. Here is an example of a statement that might be included on a syllabus:

> *Diverse Perspectives.* Participation includes self- and peer-assessment of your contributions to creating and sustaining a collaborative learning environment. Therefore, in your final response paper of the semester you are asked to describe two learning situations you experienced during this course: a) one time when you were influenced/persuaded by the insights of one of your peers, and b) one time when your comments influenced/persuaded the thinking of one of your peers.

The act of writing out such goals clarifies the knowledge, values, and skills you bring to the teaching endeavor as well.

INSTRUCTOR SELF-AWARENESS

Self-awareness as an instructor is key to understanding diverse views. An actual example may illustrate the challenge.

Consider how the content of a student presentation caught a well-respected, experienced white male instructor by surprise. Most of the students in his class were white except for several African Americans. The instructor assigned presentations on images from popular culture to students in his communication class. During class presentations, an all-white student group displayed an image that had been widely circulated on socially conservative Internet sites depicting then presidential candidate Barack Obama lynched. The presentation shocked two African American students who did not know what to say at the time. The instructor felt uncomfortable with the image, but did not say anything at the time. When asked later, he acknowledged that he had been uncomfortable with the image; but he worried that if he interrupted the presentation, he would appear to censor students' voices. In retrospect, he recognized that his personal experiences, professional training, and commitment to freedom of speech had shaped his response. (He had been deeply involved in the student freedom of speech movement on college campuses during the 1960s.)

After class, two African American students talked to a staff member of the school's multicultural student support office. This staff member then contacted the instructor to convey the students' concerns. The professor arranged a talk with the students immediately. He apologized, shared his discomfort with the image at the time, and expressed regret for not taking immediate action. Next, the instructor spoke to the students who brought in the image to explore their motives. The students were surprised and apologetic about the negative responses. The instructor felt the students' actions, while clearly insensitive, did not warrant disciplinary action. However, he realized that he needed to organize a class discussion to address the sensitive issues the presentation raised.

The instructor began the next class with a brief, informal writing assignment. Students responded to the questions, "What thoughts and feelings came up for you during the presentation that used the image of Obama lynched? What thoughts or feelings related to the image have surfaced for you since that class?" Next, he had students divide into pairs and share their perspectives with each other. Later, he led the whole class in a discussion of the historical meaning and symbolism of lynching.

When you confront an in-class incident that you do not feel prepared to handle, consult your department head and colleagues. They can help you identify the core learning issues, anticipate the range of possible student responses, and clarify university policies. These strategies lay the foundation for the trust and sustained engagement that will encourage students to engage you and your students more deeply later on.

UNDERSTANDING OUR STUDENTS

Establishing effective relationships with students in your course is central to inclusive teaching. Sometimes, social and cultural differences between students and teachers lead to unintended consequences such as missed, or misunderstood, social cues. Such miscommunications can also lead to alienation from the classroom. A typical way for students of European ancestry to signal their instructors that they would like a chance to speak is to make sustained eye contact, raise their hand, or jump in at the first lull in conversation. For first generation college attendees, Latino/Latina students, and Native American heritage students, such behaviors may be equivalent to exhibiting disrespect for the teacher. They may wait for you to call on or specifically invite them to participate. A useful strategy is to make it common practice to reserve time in free-flowing discussions for students who have not spoken yet to get easy access to the floor.

Another useful strategy for building an inclusive classroom is to ask appropriate questions. A common practice is to ask students to complete a survey on the first day of class. Such surveys can ask students about other courses they may have taken in preparation for this one, what they think might be most difficult for them in the course, what they want you to know about them as learners, and their interests in the topic beyond the specific course goals. To ascertain how wide-ranging your students' perspectives are, include questions that ask them to describe their diversity-related experiences such as study abroad, out-of-state vacations, or distinctive attributes of their families (e.g., a gay or lesbian relative). Some instructors solicit such information in discussions on the first day of class as a way to help students get to know each other. However, this can backfire, as demonstrated in the following example. An instructor in anthropology was encouraging his students to share their experiences of diversity on the first day of class. He asked students a series of questions, but no one volunteered to talk. Feeling desperate, he asked if anyone had ever traveled out of state. At that question, a young man's hand shot up, and he said that he had just returned from Iraq. The teacher asked him what he had noticed about Iraq or the Iraqi people he met, and the student responded, "The men hold hands in the street, and they all smell." The student's comment complicated and redirected a discussion the instructor hoped would promote casual community building. Before you get to know your students, you cannot predict what stories they will relate or how they will interpret the experiences. Therefore, the recommendation is that you first have students write out their responses so that you can review their answers and decide how to proceed.

Practices that support inclusion goals include knowing your students' names. If you get a student's name wrong, ask the student to correct your pronunciation and practice it until you get it right. This practice models for students how to seek out information respectfully from each other in the classroom setting that might otherwise feel awkward.

A comprehensive syllabus is essential for students with a range of needs. You can distribute your syllabus in print format, give an oral presentation, and discuss it on the first day of class. Supplement these efforts with an electronic version available online. Students may need to access the information contained in the syllabus a number of times and in a range of formats. The electronic version allows students with visual disabilities to open the file in a variety of enhanced formats (e.g., large print) or, for students with hearing challenges, have it read into an audio file by support staff. As the semester unfolds, students who may speak English as a second language or students with attention deficit disorders benefit from regular verbal instructions that refer back to the syllabus.

Students with Disabilities

Students who come to campus with identified disabilities generally establish relationships with campus service providers immediately. Gaining an understanding of the roles of academic support staff on campus is essential for you, too. One way to communicate your support for students who request accommodations is to include a statement on your syllabus. Here is an example:

> The university is committed to providing an equal educational opportunity for all students. If you have a documented physical, psychological, or learning disability on file with Disability Services (DS), Learning Disabilities Support Services (LDSS), or Psychological Disabilities

Services (PDS), you may be eligible for reasonable academic accommodations to help you succeed in this course. If you have a documented disability that requires an accommodation, please notify me within the first two weeks of the semester so that we may make appropriate arrangements early in the semester.

Such a statement communicates your commitment to appropriate support for students and your awareness of institutional procedures.

Staff members can help you quickly become familiar with what accommodations are appropriate for particular students' needs. They can also help you connect students with the appropriate student service offices in a timely manner. For example, offices disabilities normally provide instructors and students with a range of brief Web-based guides to understanding different disabilities. One guide may explain that visually impaired students benefit from access to printed materials in alternative formats (e.g., books on tape, readers). A different guide may explain that students with hearing disabilities may require note-taking services, sign language interpreters, or oral transliterators (a person who silently mouths a paraphrase so that a student who reads lips can more easily follow along).

Most accommodations are easy to implement with proper notice. These may include extended time on exams, additional time to complete assignments, alternative types of evaluation procedures, help with note taking, and access to prepared materials before class. Beyond personal values and commitments to inclusive teaching, institutions and instructors have a legal responsibility to provide appropriate accommodations mandated for students who have complied with federal, state, and institutional documentation requirements.

Instructional technologies have made accommodations far easier to access for students with disabilities. It is likely that your institution has an office dedicated to assistive technologies that may include access to scanners, optical character recognition software, reading software, text enlargers, and other devices. Often such offices work collaboratively with librarians and academic technology offices to address a range of classroom-based needs such as paying students to be note takers, using scanners to enlarge images, or increasing font sizes for students with visually impairments. Similarly, recording texts makes them accessible to students with reading- and comprehension-related challenges.

Students with documented learning or physical disabilities are often aware of the support they will need to do well in your course. Such students will often contact you directly, either before the course begins or on the first day of classes, to make appropriate arrangements. To support communication, offer students a variety of ways to contact you with questions such as text, phone, and e-mail addresses. If you have a course Web site, many learning management systems (e.g., Blackboard) have a built-in course e-mail system students can use to contact you. Some students with new disabilities (e.g., veterans) may be reluctant to disclose their needs to others because of prior expectations that they need to keep any vulnerabilities secret. Others may have been able to manage the demands of classes at the high school level with some success by hiding their struggles. At the college level, however, the scholastic challenges rise significantly. Once writing assignments begin to become past due or readings pile up, students may better accept the evidence that they need help. Cuing students about their progress with mid-semester status progress reports and, if they are failing, requiring them to come talk with you can be useful strategies to engage students in an honest assessment of their progress to date. Students struggling with learning disabilities (undiagnosed or not) may feel shame, frustration, or loss of self-confidence because their best efforts are failing. It is important to reiterate your commitments to helping students succeed and supporting their engagement with services for support.

In our increasingly "24/7" access to electronic communication, spelling out in the syllabus when and how often you expect to collect and respond to such communications can help head off conflicts between you and your students. Providing these guidelines also encourages help-seeking behaviors for all students. Inform them of campus-wide and departmental resources, coach them on how and when to use office hours or tutorial services, and, perhaps most importantly, normalize these behaviors.

Veterans

Due to American engagements in recent armed conflicts and wars, colleges and universities in the United States have increasing numbers of veterans on campus today and expect even more in the next decade. The

Post-9/11 GI Bill and the U.S. Department of Veterans Affairs (VA) currently provide the most significant education benefits for veterans (e.g., a full scholarship to any state institution) since the original GI Bill. Over 570,000 veterans are in classrooms on college on university campuses today, and this number will continue to grow. Most veterans make a seamless transition to campus life, but instructors will be better prepared if they understand how the gap between campus and military life and the onset of new psychological or physical disabilities may create challenges for some veterans.

As with any other demographic group, some veterans will have had preexisting physical or learning disabilities prior to service. However, a unique aspect of the experiences of soldiers who served active duty in Iraq, Afghanistan, or Kuwait is that they are more likely to survive injuries that proved lethal in the past due to changes in equipment and health care provision. A record number of veterans are returning to civilian life with the loss of limbs or mild brain injuries (MBI) that would have proven deadly in earlier conflicts. For example, a residual result from concussive blasts may leave some veterans struggling with MBI. Assignments that require a large amount of memorization may be problematic. They may benefit from coaching on how to use mnemonics or other strategies to increase their memory. Other veterans may have physical impairments, such as the loss of an arm or a leg, which may make accessibility to classrooms and buildings and to physical activities in the course (e.g., labs, field trips, and studio assignments) difficult.

As an instructor, you can offer important academic support in helping veterans navigate campus bureaucracies and the Department of Veterans Affairs by linking them to appropriate campus-based services. More than 20 percent of college campuses today offer veterans an orientation course specifically designed to offer academic mentoring and emotional support.

Some veterans may struggle with the informality and individualism of classroom settings, especially early on in their transition. The switch from close-knit, group-oriented activities to independent decision making and individual performance can be a challenge. Across all branches of service, military environments are hierarchical. Servicemen and servicewomen often form intense relationships in their subcommunities (units, platoons, squads, or crews) that prize solidarity and cohesion. In addition, their purpose is universally clear: service to the mission. In the military, the ability to adhere to these attributes may be the difference between success and catastrophic failure such as loss of life. In classrooms, veterans may initially feel isolated and out-of-sync with other students because of the significant differences in life experiences, nontraditional age, and other residual consequences of duty. Additionally, veterans may be apprehensive about how instructors and peers will respond to their experiences and perspectives.

Some veterans will return to civilian life with new disabilities, compromised health, or psychological vulnerabilities. It is projected that as many as a quarter of veterans will have hidden disabilities, such as traumatic brain injury (TBI), posttraumatic stress disorder (PTSD), and other emotional disorders. Others still will have visible or invisible physical disabilities, such as loss or impairment of limbs, eyes, or hearing. In addition, certain disabilities may take time to develop, and even the student may not easily recognize the effects of such disabilities for a time. Therefore, some students (e.g., those with TBI) may not know the full extent of their limitations until they are back in classes. Because they may not have needed services prior to enlistment, some veterans are unaware of their rights as students with disabilities, which can slow them down in seeking help. In addition, some will have negative feelings about disclosing a disability since military culture stigmatizes vulnerability.

Instructors can reach out and offer support useful to all students and essential for veterans who have been away from the classroom setting for a time. For example, such students would benefit from instruction in college-level reading strategies and note-taking skills. Some veterans may need extra support in learning the conventions of academic writing, which are often quite different from military-style writing. Break writing assignments down into components and offer multiple opportunities for feedback. Veterans may particularly appreciate opportunities to participate in peer editing or other collaborative-learning assignments.

Some veterans with PTSD may have strong feelings about where they feel comfortable sitting in class. On occasion, they may need to get up and leave the class quickly because of anxiety. For example, veterans report that after returning to civilian life it can take a while to let go of being "on point." This can lead to overresponsiveness to loud noises or particular alertness to strangers.

Veterans with spinal cord injuries or amputations may find tasks requiring physical dexterity (e.g., labs, computer- or writing-based assignments, and prolonged sitting or standing) challenging. Veteran students with hearing impairments may face difficulty hearing accurately in lectures or participating actively in discussion sections. Students with visual impairments may require accommodations to be able to see the board or easily resized course materials in electronic formats. Veterans with MBI may struggle with tasks that require short-term memory, sustained attention, or speedy processing of new information. Anxiety, irritability, impatience, and misreading social cues in the classroom may be a result of stress-related psychological conditions.

Despite these adjustments, veterans are not all dealing with PTSD symptoms. Veterans have a great deal to contribute to classrooms, and recognition of their service and support in the transition to college life can be rewarding for all.

International Students

Increasingly, international students are coming to the United States for undergraduate education. For some, this is their first undergraduate experience, but for others their second, some having already completed a degree in their home country. Clearly, international students have a wide range of goals and levels of readiness for learning in an American classroom. Use the activities outlined above to help international students feel welcome in the classroom. Additionally, you are also likely to discover a number of offices and support services specifically for international students. A quick survey of these resource providers and their roles on campus will help prepare you to better answer students' questions, direct them to appropriate service providers, and identify people that can answer your questions.

Pedagogical practices in American higher education encourage students to actively engage in discussions. Asking and/or responding to questions from you or other students is often the way teachers assess student engagement. But asking an instructor questions or engaging in a dialogue is discouraged in many foreign education systems. Some international students perceive questioning the instructor as rude or disrespectful, so it is important to draw them into discussions. International students may not be comfortable enough with English yet to participate in a free-form conversation. Asking students to pair up and respond to some guided questions can help students practice conversational skills. Alternatively, asking students to complete a brief writing assignment and then share their work with the class helps English as a second language (ESL) students more easily communicate their ideas.

To some international students, American classrooms can seem inordinately informal, even rude. Students coming to class in slippers or putting their feet up on chairs would be unheard of in other cultures. Providing all students with a quick review of expectations can help everyone feel more comfortable. Talking about forms of address acceptable to you and your expectations about the level of formality in class can be especially important. Some international students will find a middle ground, such as referring to you as "Professor Michael," creating a fusion of formal and informal modes of address.

Some foreign students may have difficulty understanding you initially, especially if you speak quickly. It is important to be explicit and, when possible, to provide visual aids such as PowerPoint slides containing key terms or models. In the same vein, you may have difficulty in understanding some students as well. It is important to ask the students to repeat themselves until you understand clearly what they are saying. In these situations, always communicate your desire to understand the student and work at it until you do. These issues, and others such as accents, are often dependent on how long the student has been in the United States. It is important not to let feelings of self-consciousness or of embarrassment lead you to give up too quickly. You should encourage other students to do the same.

Talking with students before or after class can be an opportunity to discover what international students know about the content of the course. Ask students what they have or have not learned before so that they can adjust their teaching plan accordingly. Some international students may not be able quickly to discern and articulate what they do or do not know. They may simply say, "I don't know," rather than hold up the class. International students may also be self-conscious about losing "face," or being embarrassed, if unsure whether other students know material they do not. Don't make adjustments to the course to help one or two students. But do what you can to aid students who are struggling.

To assess language skills, have students break into small groups to share their cultural backgrounds by responding to open-ended questions. An alternative is to ask students early on in the course to complete brief in-class writing assignments. Multiple, low-risk assignments can give you a great deal of insight into students' writing and comprehension skills. These exercises could include creating posters, brochures, poems, or movie reviews. These assignments also enable you to ascertain a student's comfort and proficiency in talking with peers. All students will benefit from opportunities to receive early feedback on drafts of assignments and submit revisions. If you choose to respond to students' use of grammar, comment selectively and specifically early on in the assignment and then encourage students to check the rest of their work for similar errors. This approach has the benefit of not overwhelming or intimidating international students.

In the same way that providing disabled students with options for completing graded assignments has proven useful, consider offering international students the option of doing take-home exams or bringing desktop references to class during exams. For example, you might encourage any student who wishes to utilize resources like a dictionary or thesaurus.

Multiculturally Inclusive Content

Even instructors who do not explicitly identify multicultural learning goals as central to their course may still find that diversity becomes an important component of the teaching and learning process. Some such opportunities happen spontaneously.

Recently, a young white female instructor taught an undergraduate anthropology course at a local community college. She had taught the course a number of times before at the university level and was excited to bring it to new students. Of the twenty-five students in the course, twenty-two were Latino or mixed race. All of the students were from an urban New England city, and most of the students spoke Spanish as their first language.

The instructor assigned a book on homelessness written by a noted anthropologist who is an expert on root causes of homelessness in contemporary societies. Although the author lives in England, the instructor arranged a presentation via Skype (an online teleconferencing software).

On the day of the class the technology worked flawlessly, the guest presenter was well prepared, students were attentive and actively engaged through the entire presentation, and the author handled the question and answer time with respect and humor. At the conclusion of the presentation, a robust conversation continued between students. Finally, the instructor felt compelled to end the discussion so that she could allow the class to have a regularly schedule break and then move on to other topics.

She called on a student but prefaced his comment with a statement like "let's hear from so-and-so and that will be the last comment before we move on to our break." As that student made his comment, the instructor noticed another student angrily pile his books up on his desk and rush out of the classroom saying loudly as he left, "this is bullshit." During the break, he revealed to her that his family had lived in homeless shelters off-and-on during his childhood. Before the discussion ended, he wanted to share some of his experiences. She reassured him that they would return to the discussion and encouraged him to come back to class and share his perspectives.

In the next class, a young Latina woman emotionally volunteered to the class that her father was chronically homeless when she was young. She went on to share that it was not until she read this book that she understood his experiences with homelessness. She started to cry, telling the class that her father had died a few years before and that she wished that she had read this book sooner, so she would have known how to talk to him.

Although the instructor had expected to move on, she realized the current topic remained important to her students. Some students were clearly struggling personally with a range of emotional responses to the material and to the new insights into their families' lives. She had not anticipated that the material would have such personal resonance for some of her students, until she noticed the emotional cues of her two students and responded compassionately. All of the students in the class benefited from hearing about the experiences of their peers. Their stories became anchors for the academic research and theoretical models.

This example offers some general guidelines for creating an inclusive classroom. First, if an unexpected event or comment occurs in class, do not feel like you must have a definitive response to it immediately. It may not be clear to you what the best way is to intervene in the moment, and you may want to consult with other instructors or students to get more perspectives.

Some situations, however, require that you simply stop inappropriate behaviors or communications. For example, respond immediately to comments that are obviously offensive and run counter to civility (e.g., openly racist or homophobic remarks). If you do not act, you risk losing the trust of the rest of the class. You will be the best judge of how direct to be in responding to a student. In such an instance, your response might range from saying, "That comment was hard to hear because . . ." to "That comment is entirely out of line and unacceptable. Please apologize now."

If the comment was an unintentional or unconscious expression, you may try to turn it into a learning opportunity. For example, if a student makes a controversial comment, you can begin by asking students for other perspectives on the topic. Once you have elicited several perspectives out, you can return to the original student's comment and link the discussion to the general discussion that does not put the individual student in the position of defending it. For example, "John said he believes, as do other people, that . . . How might people come to hold such a perspective?"

In these "hot moments," it is important to be firm while keeping the overall tension in the atmosphere low. It is all right to be frustrated but not all right to be explosive or punitive. In the incident described above, the instructor did not intentionally seek to insert diversity into the content of her course, and yet her experience helped her to point out that whether or not we see diversity as a formal part of our curriculum, it is always a part of the informal context of learning. As you become more experienced, you will begin to be more comfortable and more adept at using these moments as powerful and spontaneous opportunities for learning.

Moving Forward

Instructors may initially face a quagmire of preconceptions about multiculturalism and inclusive teaching. You should reject such preconceptions "diversity is a factor in only some disciplines," "fairness is treating all students exactly the same," "only diversity experts can address multicultural issues," "emotions in the classroom mean loss of control," and "accommodations for students lessens the rigor of the course."

To assess the general level of inclusivity of your course, begin by making sure your content reflects diverse perspectives. Find and assign the work of a range of scholars from underrepresented groups in your discipline. Also, make it clear to students that the value of these scholars' contributions to the discipline extends beyond their social identities. Examine your course materials to ascertain whether they employ gender-neutral language, diverse examples, and culturally inclusive illustrations.

As you create assignments and assessment tools, provide students with a variety of ways to learn and demonstrate their mastery of the core material. Offer students access to course materials in accessible formats. Value the affective aspects of learning by rewarding students' self-awareness, personal growth, and change as outcomes of the learning process. Finally, avoid the trap of feeling compelled to be universally expert on everything. Balance your strengths by inviting guest speakers with expertise and experiences different from your own.

The guidelines in this chapter lay a positive foundation for creating an inclusive teaching and learning environment in courses across the disciplines. By understanding and responding to the needs of a diverse groups of students, instructors can incorporate practices that ultimately benefit all students. As you reflect on how your experiences and values shape your approach to teaching and learning, experiment with new strategies in the classroom that will create an environment where all of your students can truly reach their potential.

Using Electronic Resources for Teaching

Computers and related electronic resources play a significant role in education. Most of your students will have considerable experience with the Internet and will, whether you like it or not, make use of it for much of their academic work. Many of them are accustomed to using e-mail as a normal form of communication, as well as newer forms such as instant messaging and social networking. But teachers can benefit from these electronic resources as well by employing a series of useful tools. We stress the word "useful" because technology complements, but seldom replaces, more conventional teaching techniques. Electronic tools can make classes more efficient; lectures more compelling, informative, and varied; reading assignments more extensive, interesting, and accessible; discussions more free ranging and challenging; and students' papers more original and well researched. Only you, however, can judge if technology truly enhances your teaching.

Five Promising Uses of New Technology

Of the many electronic teaching techniques that instructors have found useful, five seem particularly likely to help significant numbers of teachers perform common and routine tasks. All of these techniques demand an investment of time if they are to succeed, and you will need to balance your willingness to use them against other, perhaps more important, teaching priorities. For each technique, moreover, there are both simple and complex ways of proceeding, and we will try to make clear the respective advantages and disadvantages. Nevertheless, we are confident that new technologies can and will help you do your difficult and demanding job more effectively and easily.

- *Administration:* A learning management system (LMS) such as Blackboard, WebCT, or Moodle makes advertising a class, providing copies of the syllabus, assigning discussion sections, and getting out course news far more efficient. So too can a self-published course home page. These tools can also dramatically improve the continuity and community aspects of courses, helping students to engage with and learn from each other and even from people outside the course.

- *Readings/sources/experiments:* The Web and CD-ROMs provide a wider variety of online readings, primary sources, and raw data (including visual and audio sources), as well as interactive experiments and models than has previously been available. With your guidance, students can now gain access to materials that were once accessible only to experts because they were too cumbersome to reproduce for classroom use or too expensive for students to purchase. Moreover, by discovering sources on their own, students can bring unique pieces of evidence and arguments into lectures and discussions, as well as write on a wider range of research topics. Many research libraries also make available access to academic journals online as well as many complete digitized books, all of which you can assign to your students, usually at no cost to them or you.

- *Papers/presentations:* Rather than receiving assignments and taking exams from the teacher alone, students can perform more independent exercises in assembling, publishing, and presenting research findings, teaching units, and other materials for their peers. A Web archive that contains the work product of several terms can transform the course into an ongoing and collaborative intellectual endeavor.

- *Lectures:* A computer with presentation software can augment lectures with outlines, slides, statistical charts and tables, images, music, and video clips. In addition to printing them as handouts, you can save in-class presentations in a Web-compatible format for later review and discussion.

- *Discussion:* Tools such as e-mail, discussion boards, conferencing software, and online chat services can seed questions before the class meets, draw out your shy students, promote follow-up exchanges, and facilitate additional questions on the reading between classes. For courses without face-to-face discussion sections, these resources can bring the course to life over great distances and help overcome scheduling difficulties.

In the sections below, we discuss each of these techniques and how you might consider using them.

The Necessary Tools

What you need will depend, of course, on what you want to do. Most teachers have computers, and most have at least some access to e-mail and the Internet. In nearly all schools and universities, your students do, too. Many teaching resources are undoubtedly already available to you, using equipment you and your students presently have. But other techniques require more advanced technologies that you may or may not wish to purchase on your own, and that your institution may or may not make available to you. It is important, therefore, that you make no plans for using electronic tools before confirming that both you and your students will have access to the necessary technology. It is especially important to make no assumptions about computer access that might penalize lower-income students, adding to their workloads through long waits at the computer lab or delayed receipt of classroom updates or assignments—although many schools and universities supply low-income students with computers and see them as necessary tools for education.

But owning, or having access to, technology is usually only a first step. Even more critical is learning how to use it. This is one of the biggest challenges facing anyone who wishes to use electronic tools, because the knowledge is not always easy to acquire. Many teachers, of course, are highly skilled in computer technology and know how to teach themselves to do almost anything. But many others have limited computer skills, are easily intimidated by new and unfamiliar tasks, and tend to avoid doing anything that requires them to learn something very different from what they already know. If you fall in the latter group but wish to expand your ability to use electronic tools, you need to find help. Some institutions offer extensive assistance through their computer centers or their information technology services. Some departments have staff members or graduate student assistants who are hired to handle computer-related problems. There are also many excellent reference works to help you learn about various electronic tools. Having access to the necessary help—in whatever form it takes—is just as important as having access to the necessary technology when it comes to using electronic resources in the classroom.

Keep in mind, finally, that the technology associated with computers and the Internet changes with breathtaking speed. This is a vital source of useful innovation. But the rapidity of change can be bewildering and intimidating. Although certain skills will remain useful to you over long periods of time, many others will have to be relearned time and time again. To avoid problems later, it is wise to make a quick inventory of your own and your school's electronic teaching resources before you decide to introduce new teaching techniques. You will not want to discover halfway through a project that there are major obstacles such as insufficient equipment, inadequate support, or negative professional incentives. Posing a few simple questions to colleagues, administrators, librarians, and specialists in advance can help you determine how practical and promising potential innovations in electronic teaching are likely to be.

- What teaching resources are available from your school's Web site? What courses have material online? Which departments and faculty have Web pages? How are they constructed and updated? Where are they stored? (One source for help in understanding how your institution's Web site works is the office or team in charge of maintaining the school Web site. If your school has a Web site, look at the bottom of the home page or on the credits page of the site to find the contact information for this office.)
- What kinds of computers and Internet access do students have? Do most students own their own computers? If not, are there long waits for access? Twenty-four-hour computer labs? Provisions for off-campus students?
- Does your school recommend or support any particular software for Web pages? For presentations, word processing, spreadsheets, and databases? What software is on the public campus computers? For example, can you assume everyone can open a Microsoft

Word document? Does it matter whether you use Office 2003 or 2007 or whatever new editions will inevitably appear? And what Internet browser (and version) do students typically use?

- Has your school installed a LMS that offers simple fill-in-the-blank online forms to allow you to place standard course material on the Internet, after which the program creates the course home page for you? If not, is there a school style sheet or recommended format for course pages?

- What staff is available to assist instructors with educational technology? Are there any work-study students or teaching assistants trained for new media support? What handouts or online guides have been prepared for electronic teaching? Are there workshops for faculty who want to learn about new technologies and resources?

- Are there particular classrooms designed for multimedia presentations? Which classrooms have Internet access? Does the campus have reliable, pervasive wireless Internet access, or are some classrooms "dead zones" where a wired connection might still be required? Are classes that are making use of this technology given extra technical or financial support? Are the "smart" classrooms only available to certain instructors?

- Are there special funds or professional recognition for innovative uses of technology in teaching? Are any of your colleagues working on grants that support electronic teaching? What is the attitude of your department and of school officials to this activity?

- Does your institution have distance learning plans (methods by which students with online access can take courses remotely)? How is your department's teaching and funding going to be affected by these plans?

- What can you use on the Internet? Even though the Internet is now more than twenty years old, its rapidly evolving delivery systems still do not yet have clear guidelines for determining fair use and copyright policies for online teaching materials. In general, however, the same copyright rules that govern photocopied packets and other, more familiar teaching tools are likely to apply to online material. You should, however, identify the office or officer at your institution responsible for monitoring such policies, starting perhaps with the reserve desk at the library where many students go for their nontextbook course readings.

- Will your online materials belong to you? Investigate your institution's policies (or ask for one to be made) on whether you or the school owns your online materials. This is especially important if you are investing considerable creative time and energy or making heavy use of university equipment and staff. What happens to the materials you create if you move to another academic institution? Can you commercially publish material developed for an online course at a later date, or does the university own the copyright? Can another professor use your course materials to teach the same course?

The Course Web Site

When the World Wide Web first became popular on campuses, professors sought to take advantage of this new technology by constructing their own course home pages. This often involved learning the language of basic Web publishing, hypertext markup language (HTML), or one of a variety of programs that hid some of the details of HTML behind an interface similar to a word processor. Once the page was composed, you still faced a sometimes baffling series of highly technical steps to make the material visible on the campus network. In the past, many teachers became proficient in these technologies. But today most institutions have taken steps to eliminate the technical challenges to creating, organizing, and adding content to a course Web site through a LMS.

While an online course site is often optional, at many institutions a simple online outline for the course is created automatically or by filling out a simple request form with information services or tech support. Your first task is to determine whether or not to make use of it and, if so, to what extent. A course Web site can serve several functions. Even before the course begins, it can advertise your course to prospective students. Before and during the term it can reduce demand for paper copies of print materials such as the syllabus, assignments, and study questions. While traditional paper-based readings can be uploaded to the site, most systems can also present a broader range of material including multimedia sources such as video and audio as well as links to more elaborate items hosted on other Web sites on or off campus. As the name implies, a course home page can act as a twenty-four-hour communications center for news, assignments, and discussions. Indeed, it can play host to the four other electronic techniques discussed below.

Like all parts of a course, you should first define carefully the scope and content of the Web site. It is best to start simply and enhance your site in stages to benefit from experience and feedback. The simplest sites consist of a single page reproducing the traditional paper syllabus. The next, more useful level includes separate pages or sections for paper assignments, section lists, and hyperlinks to readings and sources. The most advanced sites, such as those for distance learning courses, can include all the materials needed for the course: lectures, readings, audio and video recordings, exams, and evaluations. Do not underestimate the technical knowledge, time, and energy required to keep these more advanced pages up to date and err on the side of caution your first semester. Students will accept any of these levels of Web presence as a convenience, but become disoriented and disappointed if the performance does not match the promise as the term continues.

As with most projects, a good outline and clear definition of your Web site can save many hours of false starts and hasty revisions. Here are a few basic questions to ask before you start:

- What are the goals of your site? Is it going to perform administrative chores? Advertise the course? Introduce unique materials? Publish and archive student work? Answers to these questions should shape the design and scope of your site.
- What are the features you like and dislike about existing course sites at your school and on the Internet? What institutional support, standards, and tools might guide your efforts?
- What traditional materials will go on the site? Your syllabus, assignments, handouts, bibliographies, slides, maps?
- What multimedia or otherwise cumbersome material might a Web page easily include? Sound recordings, images, video, statistical data?
- Which of your readings are available or could be made available online? Are there reputable Internet sources on a particular topic? Can you scan material into your site without violating copyright

laws? If students print out these resources because of their length or complexity, is there a more economical or ecologically friendly way to deliver them? Will the home page host student publications, lecture materials, or online discussions? What is the time commitment involved in monitoring and participating in each of these activities for you and for the student? Which of these items is essential to meeting your goals? Which could be saved for a second, third, or fourth stage of development? Which have little educational value and should be dropped?

- What are logical divisions for all of this course material? Web sites should usually limit their menus to fewer than ten choices to insure students can easily and efficiently navigate the site.

When you decide to create a course site, you will have a number of methods from which to choose. Most likely, your school will provide an instructor-only username and password for administering the site. Ready-made categories such as Course Information, Assignments, Discussion Board, and Quizzes may already be created for you. The task then is to copy and paste your course syllabi and assignments into the appropriate forms. If possible, try to upload easily printable versions of your syllabus and other materials in Adobe's portable document format (PDF) or the nearly universal rich text format (RTF) or Microsoft Word as file attachments using the appropriate buttons and prompts for your LMS. If there are glitches in the appearance of your materials, you may have to get help from someone on campus who is expert at transferring material from word processing files to a Web-compatible format; in this case, prepare the material using a word processor, making sure to use simple formatting that will translate easily to the Web. (Italics and bold are best; underlining can be confused with hyperlinks and is less common online.) Then give it to whoever is transferring the material to your Web site. If you are constructing the Web page yourself, look for assistance—in computer manuals or from a knowledgeable colleague or student—in using the various editing tools available.

The most successful course Web sites use the unique capabilities of the medium to provide material not available to students in other forms. This could include links to online readings, lecture outlines, or even sample exam questions that are not otherwise distributed to the class.

Or, if your school's software allows, you could use your course Web site to view video clips, audio recordings, interactive experiments, or complex models that formerly might have required logistically difficult group visits to a computer lab.

Whether you have used your institution's LMS software, constructed your own Web site, or had someone else do it for you, you should proofread your pages carefully, test to make sure all the links work, and keep a careful eye on the overall size of pages and images. Because Web sites often look different on various computers, you should also try to view your pages in as many different browsers as possible, especially in the Macintosh and Windows computer labs that the students might be using. If you have students who commute to campus, try to get access to your course materials from off campus with ordinary broadband and, if your region or student population makes it likely, even a telephone-based modem to ensure that computers not directly connected to your institution's network can display your pages and graphics efficiently. Few things in life are more aggravating than waiting for an image to load on a computer with a slow Internet connection.

Once you have constructed a Web site, make an effort to publicize it. Be sure that it is listed in all the proper places on your school's Web site—that there are clear links to it from, for example, your department's home page. Put the site's Internet address (known as a URL) on your paper course materials. Describe the site to your students on the first few days of class, write the URL on the board, and indicate whether and where they can get technical assistance.

Electronic Readings and Sources

For the moment, at least, most traditionally printed textbooks and monographs have not been replaced by digital readers or online versions. Students and faculty have often balked at reading long passages of text on a computer screen. Nonetheless, as the economics of electronic publishing builds momentum and the technology for displaying text on screens improves, the student backpack will almost certainly contain fewer printed books and more electronic devices for efficiently accessing digital reading assignments. But even if the primary textbooks remain printed for many more years, classrooms can often benefit from electronic resources in at least two areas: supplementary readings and primary sources. Even the best published readers or photocopied packets tend to dampen the thrill of discovery because they have been preselected and packaged for a particular purpose (seldom your own). Electronic sources, whether on CD-ROM or the Web, can significantly broaden the range of materials accessible to your students.

There are a wide variety of electronic resources that can be useful for the classroom. Among the most popular have been CD-ROM document collections such as *Chaucer: Life and Times; Pennsylvania Gazette, 1728–1783;* and *Presidential Papers: Washington–Clinton.* Textbook publishers are increasingly providing electronic study guides, map exercises, sample presentation slides, and computerized test banks on CD-ROM, flash drives, or on the Web. Some schools are producing, or arranging access to, large collections of digital materials that students can access from within their campus networks, but are not usually indexed by popular Web search engines such as Google. While more and more material is available through Web browsers, do not forget to check for these proprietary or seemingly dated formats such as CD-ROMs, which might contain just what students need for a project. This is especially true for materials that would be too costly or impossible to license for global Internet access, but have proven affordable for the more limited and measurable publication of CD-ROMs or paid subscriptions.

While by no means the only source of information, the Internet has emerged as the most extensive, and ever expanding, source for electronic resources. Many Web sites can deliver an astounding array of primary documents, secondary literature, sound, and images. Students who explore Web sites related to a course can bring compelling evidence and arguments back to the class. Publishers are building companion Web sites around their textbooks, and large international projects have been launched to provide online sources for standard humanities, natural science, and social science survey courses. Finally, libraries, companies like Google, and scholarly projects are making scanned materials accessible over the Web, although the copyright implications of this practice require close attention. Campus libraries also typically subscribe to dozens of online databases such as PubMed, JSTOR, or governmental data clearinghouses with full-text articles from scholarly journals, newspapers, statistical data sets, and manuscript collections.

In all these cases, the relatively new forms of material require some special handling. As you begin to select electronic sources for your course, bear in mind the following guidelines:

- Ensure that all electronic assignments contribute directly to the objectives of the course. The new materials should pass the same relevance test as traditional material.
- Evaluate the scholarly quality of the electronic sources. Although linking to electronic sources might be free, one substandard source can lower the credibility of the course.
- Use the appropriate medium. Can these materials be more easily or effectively used in a more traditional form? Try to use the Web for things that it can do particularly well: displaying multimedia material, hyperlinking to other sources, providing interactive experiences, or improving access to otherwise cumbersome or distant materials. As more and more online archives afford access to recordings and radio and television programs, the value of online assignments can only rise. But sometimes a printed handout or a photocopy packet is a more economical and ecological choice.
- When dealing with larger collections of primary documents, make the task of using them more manageable by discussing ahead of time the particular questions the collection might help answer. Then divide the class into groups, each of which will explore the archive with a particular question in mind. Short review papers, Web page postings, or in-class presentations can enable each group to share small numbers of documents, images, and other artifacts that address the question or theme they have chosen.
- Reinforce traditional research skills. Using online information requires at least as much skill and discipline as using traditional sources. Just because students can "cut and paste" from online sources, the process of researching and writing is not fundamentally different from a project that uses more traditional sources. Encourage students to take the same detailed notes and to follow the same strict citation procedures they use for conventional printed sources.
- Mix traditional and electronic sources. Require students to consult

traditional printed and microform source material as well as electronic resources. Many valuable sources will not be digitized any time soon, if ever, so student research should include at least as many traditional sources as electronic ones. Students wedded to the Internet sometimes assume that they need never use a traditional library; some act at times as if information not on the Web does not exist. Be sure that you structure assignments in a way that does not diminish or sever the ties of your students to the most important sources of scholarly material.

- Caution your students to exercise critical judgment when making use of online sources. Explain the Web's fluid (or sometimes nonexistent) editorial standards and the need to determine the standards, origin, and scholarly discipline that went into the creation of each online source (especially Wikipedia). Virtually anyone can create a Web site, and there is no review process to test sites for accuracy or reliability unless the creator of the site initiates one. To avoid the problems such lax standards can cause, emphasize strongly the online offerings of established libraries, archives, and universities.

- Consider having students complete a quick questionnaire after reading the first electronic resource of the term so that they will become critical consumers of online material. Ask them to identify the author of the material, give the address (URL) for the site, and comment on the scholarly methods and reputation of the sponsoring organization or individual. Have them try to discover how long a site has existed and how long the reference will remain online. Will more material be added or corrections made? How should they cite this material in their papers, and how can they be sure the material will remain available at that location? A short discussion of the answers in class will counteract much of the confusion and many of the misconceptions surrounding information on the Internet. Lastly, indicate to them whether the type and quality of their sources will be an important component of their paper grade and establish clear criteria for an acceptable authority.

Multimedia Lecturing

Despite sometimes scathing criticism, lecturing remains one of the most common, and often one of the most effective, means of teaching. At its best, a lecture enlivens academic subjects with the instructor's energy and curiosity and with the persuasive nuances of human speech. Nevertheless, lecturing has its limits, most notably the reputed twelve-minute average human attention span, the difficulty of explaining complex material verbally, and the awkwardness of presenting diverse, multimedia sources with multiple pieces of often temperamental equipment.

Teachers have traditionally juggled chalkboards, whiteboards, overhead and slide projectors, and audiovisual equipment to enliven and enrich their lectures. Today, most schools provide classrooms equipped with built-in or portable multimedia computer systems, at least in the larger lecture halls. You can take advantage of the electronic possibilities for lecturing by familiarizing yourself with the most popular and powerful computerized classroom tool: presentation software such as Microsoft PowerPoint. Business presenters were the early adopters of this software. Teachers have followed in ever greater numbers and use such programs to consolidate into one device the presentation of multimedia material that supplements—not supplants—their lectures.

The basic concept behind presentation software is familiar; it is the same as that for the older and in many institutions now mostly abandoned media of slide shows or overhead transparencies. At the most elementary level, presentation programs serve as a glorified slide projector to display a sequence of pictures or documents to accompany your lecture. When using a computerized presentation, however, you can easily add captions to the images, digitally highlight or annotate them, or combine multiple images on a single "slide." Teachers who distribute lecture outlines or write them on the board might want to include that text on a projected slide, if only to spare students the need to decipher poor handwriting.

At the most advanced level, presentation programs allow teachers to add sound, video, and even interactive charts and graphs to slides. You might, for example, project a map that demonstrates various changes as you advance along a time line. If the classroom computer system has

Internet access, you can hyperlink your slides to World Wide Web resources and sites such as YouTube.com, effectively incorporating that material into your lecture.

The use of presentation software in the classroom requires careful planning and a not inconsiderable investment of time. Be prepared to take some or all of the following steps:

- Determine whether you have access to the equipment and classroom necessary to display electronic presentations. At a minimum, you will need a laptop computer, a projection device compatible with your software and hardware, and a classroom with a convenient electrical outlet, dimmable lights, and an appropriate screen. Check that the computer is capable of producing all the effects you plan for the class such as sound, video, or Internet access.
- Ensure that your own computer equipment will allow you to create and maintain these presentations. Manipulating multimedia resources such as real time video and large format images (maps, 3-D mapping) can push some laptops to their limit.
- Acquire a presentation program. Many of the more popular office suites (for instance, from Microsoft, Apple, or the open-source project OpenOffice.org) include them. Your campus may already have purchased licenses to one or more of these products. Finally, check to make sure your choice is compatible with the systems installed in classrooms.
- Write or revise your lectures with the multimedia slide show in mind. Begin to collect compelling pictures and artwork, explanatory maps and charts, music clips, even short videos that might enhance your analysis. Evaluate which of these materials can be rendered in digital form, and consider the copyright implications, especially if you plan to make your presentations available to students outside the classroom. If possible, raise any and all copyright questions with the appropriate authority in your school. When preparing text for your presentation— whether headings or explanatory captions—use simple clauses and standard fonts (for example, Arial or Times New Roman) to

ensure that your presentation will look the same regardless of what computer you are using. The best font size for headings is twenty-four point, although you can use thirty point or larger if you wish (always remember that students in the back row of the classroom will need to read whatever text you project).

- Calculate how long a visual or audio presentation will take and how much of a reduction in the other parts of your lecture may be necessary. Remember that the goal is to reinforce the main themes or issues you wish to raise—not provide students with a series of images or collection of text that will overwhelm, confuse, or stupefy them.
- Digitize the material that best advances your teaching goals. Your campus may have a central lab for digitizing materials, and you might find some of the equipment affordable enough for a department or individual to own. Make the file size of the slides as small as possible, even if it means sacrificing a little of the display quality. Students will typically experience these images and sounds on a large screen or in a noisy room, so fine details might be lost in any case.
- Keep the design of your electronic slides simple and efficient. Include only material that directly supports the point you are making in the lecture. Eliminate all unnecessary special effects, backgrounds, and animation that may distract more than inform. Do not confuse entertainment with education.
- Proofread and test your presentations thoroughly on your machine and in the classroom. Pay special attention to the legibility and overall quantity of text on your slides—less is generally more. And be sure your work is stored in at least two different places. Concentrating your multimedia material on one machine or one disk may be convenient, but this also creates a single point of failure in the notoriously fickle personal computer. External hard drives and USB storage devices (often called flash drives or thumb drives) are increasingly inexpensive options. Online storage space may also be purchased for little cost.
- Have a backup plan. Make sure that you will be able to deliver the main substance of your lecture from printed notes and, if

necessary, color transparencies whether or not everything works perfectly. In the case of equipment failure, do not waste class time trying to solve the problem.

- Plan to publish your slide shows on the course home page, if you have one and if you are confident that you have addressed any and all copyright concerns. While traditional slide shows are difficult to reproduce for absent students or to review at exam time, many presentation programs offer a relatively simple procedure for publishing your show on the Web.

- Use electronic resources to help encourage student participation during your lectures. For example, present a variety of images, primary documents, or other materials that could form the basis for an in-class debate or conversation. Some classrooms are adopting interactive "clickers" or networked devices that allow students to complete assessments, answer questions, take polls, and solve problems from their seats.

- Evaluate emerging technologies like smart-boards (white boards with integrated digital display and interactive abilities) and simulated laboratory experiments that might allow the more effective presentation of complex information.

Our final note of caution on the use of presentation software comes from Edward Tufte, whose pamphlet *The Cognitive Style of PowerPoint: Pitching Out Corrupts Within* should be required reading for all teachers planning to use presentation software. The computer screen, even when projected onto a large surface, is a relatively low-resolution device. A newspaper or a letter-sized handout can legibly display thousands of characters at once, and usually require only the simplest levels of indentation and hierarchy. Even the human voice can convey more information than the large fonts that are legible in a lecture hall over the same period of time, not to mention provide emotion, pacing, and suspense. Digital slides, encouraged by the software itself, can reduce otherwise intelligible material to a mind-numbing and sometimes downright misleading jumble of incomplete clauses, false hierarchies, and unintended juxtapositions. Use the software for material that cannot be efficiently or affordably presented through a better medium (usually print or voice). Review any text you present to make sure that it does not duplicate or replace the material you want to present to your students yourself and be on the alert for deleterious effects from the restrictions on length and the temptation to nest bullet points imposed by presentation software.

Students Using Laptops in Class

As computers have gotten more portable, powerful, and affordable, chances are an increasing number of students are bringing them into your lectures and even into discussion sections. Ostensibly, students are using these laptops to take better notes, but with pervasive wireless Internet connections their computers are capable of much more. Indeed, surveys have shown that a high percentage of these students are surfing the Web, checking their e-mail, and hopping around to various social networking sites during class. While there may be good reasons to allow students to use laptops in class, the initial studies (the bibliography lists two readings that will start you on the trail of many others) have not been encouraging about the educational impact of laptop use in class, both for the student with the laptop and for students sitting within sight of whatever is on their screen. What is to be done? Not surprisingly, faculty responses are varied, but tend to fall into three broad categories:

- Tolerate classroom laptop use by students, but educate them on the expected etiquette through the syllabus, comments at the start of the semester, and reminders (with consequences) to individuals and the group when disruptive behavior occurs. The advantage of this approach is that students are expected to govern their own behavior and adapt available technology to their learning style, whether it is a laptop, a mobile phone with keyboard, or some other recording device (assuming you permit students to tape your presentations). If all students have access to the Internet, the class as a whole might benefit from the ability to retrieve online course materials, simulations, or experiments.
- Ban or tightly control student laptop use during class, perhaps with variations that allow a small number of designated note takers or computer-equipped presentation teams to use laptops for well-defined activities. Proponents of this strategy report better student recall of class material through the summarizing and processing

that occurs when taking notes by hand. They also express a general relief at having a break from the online distractions. The students who volunteer for the roles of note taker or in-class researcher retain the freedom to use a computer in class, but have to deliver coherent notes or relevant research in the bargain.

- Embrace the decentralizing consequences of personal computers, smart phones, and other personal electronic devices and use them as the foundation for a fundamentally different style of teaching to large groups. Such teachers see Web surfing, social networking, and iPod use during lectures as, on the one hand, an unavoidable reality of future generations of students and, on the other, a rational response on the part of students to a moribund style of teaching in which information is delivered by a single instructor to passive students. Laptops offer an opportunity, according to proponents of this approach, to create in-class research teams, large-scale interactive experiments, collaborative documents or diagrams, and a more dynamic, decentralized form of learning with control of the central screen and attention of the class moving more fluidly from the professor to prepared and engaged individuals or groups.

Our advice is not to wait until the use of personal electronic devices becomes a disruption. Consider each of the strategies above and select one that most closely matches your teaching style, subject matter, and campus technology. In our experience, a combination of all of these strategies seems most promising. In sum, state clearly and firmly the etiquette and classroom policy on laptop use. Then make provisions for volunteer note takers and presentation leaders to use personal computers or smart phones. Finally, permit more extensive use of electronic equipment whenever the course material, classroom dynamic, and technical infrastructure allow you to innovate and invigorate your teaching in meaningful ways.

Electronic Discussions

Perhaps the most controversial (and probably the most common) application of technology is as a supplement to or replacement for face-to-face conversation. Small group discussions are an irreplaceable forum for teaching, learning, and thoughtful collaboration. They are not, however, without problems. Small discussion groups are an expensive way to organize teaching, and as a result they are becoming less common in some of the more budget-conscious schools and universities of our time. Some students—especially those who are shy or who are not native English speakers—are uncomfortable in small group discussions and do not actively participate in them. Students speaking in a classroom setting can make superficial contributions that would have benefited from more advance preparation. For all of these problems, online discussions can help compensate.

Online discussion tools fall into two basic categories: synchronous (chat) and asynchronous (e-mail, mailing lists, and threaded discussions). In a synchronous discussion, students in effect talk to one another over the Internet in much the same way they speak on the telephone; in asynchronous discussions, the communication is more like an exchange of letters, even if potentially much more rapid. In general, classes with no face-to-face meetings are the best candidates for synchronous online discussions that approximate the dynamic and serendipitous qualities of small discussion groups. Classes that already meet together may prefer asynchronous electronic forums as a more useful supplement to their regular discussions. An online discussion can be a good tool to ensure that students are prepared for the actual class, although your ability to read and absorb your students' work may be compromised if you use this technique for a very large group. But if the group is manageable, you might seed an online discussion by starting out the string each week with a series of questions or comments about the assigned material to which your students might respond. The most basic, but still very useful, technique is to use the campus e-mail system to broadcast messages to your students. For large lecture courses or classes that require frequent out-of-class communication, this method alone can save considerable amounts of time. Your school's LMS will almost always provide a method for sending messages to all the enrolled students, saving you the considerable effort of collecting and maintaining an accurate roster of e-mail addresses. E-mail lists—a group of e-mail addresses grouped under a single alias such as "english101" or "us-survey" and often known as a listserv—can be particularly useful for large classes. Lists can also allow members of the class to communicate with each other. Discussion boards (often included with most LMS) are threaded discussion forums that keep a permanent record of each person's contribution so that each succeeding participant can review the entire course of a conversation and add his or her own contribution to it. Chat sessions take perhaps the most planning, the most specialized software, and considerable guidance on chat room etiquette and procedures.

To use electronic discussion tools in your class, take the following steps:

- Determine whether electronic discussions contribute to your pedagogical goals. These tools require a significant time commitment from the teacher and students and should only be used if they serve an important educational function. Most teachers turn to electronic discussions to get students thinking critically about the reading before they come to class, to answer questions of comprehension and fact as they occur, to encourage consideration of a topic from multiple perspectives or roles, and to provide some continuity of thought between one week's topic and the next.
- Investigate the tools and practices of your campus. Students at most campuses in the United States are now required to maintain an e-mail address to receive official academic communications. LMS offer instructors the tools to broadcast e-mails to your class, which can work in concert with discussion boards, messaging systems, digital drop boxes, electronic office hours via instant messaging, and other student collaboration tools. Your ability to implement other forms of electronic discussions will be significantly shaped by your school's choice of additional communication tools. Social networking tools such as Facebook and Twitter, to name only two currently popular services, can also be used to engage your students, although great care must be taken to maintain a boundary between personal and professional postings and information. Only the official courseware systems of the university can guarantee that your postings are not juxtaposed and intermixed with inappropriate or unfortunate content generated by anonymous or unauthorized users. Be sure you have

a strong grasp of the quite restrictive privacy laws protecting the identities, course enrollments, and classroom submissions of your students from public exposure. While constructing a Facebook group around your course's subject matter might seem like a perfect way to win the students' hearts and minds, securing such a site from outside observers and ensuring everyone in the group is a real, authorized student registered for the course might simply be impossible.

• Make the online discussion substantive and unique. Provide information in these sessions that cannot be found elsewhere or at least not as conveniently. Online discussions can be a supplement to, or possibly a replacement for, some of the communications that occur during office hours. They can allow a student who has had a conversation with you in your office to continue that conversation with other questions and ideas as they arise; and they can allow a student who cannot attend your office hours or who was discouraged by a long line to communicate with you in other ways.

• Think of particular purposes that would be well served by electronic discussions. You might, for example, create a Web-based review session before an exam. Students can submit questions to you electronically, and you can respond to them by posting an answer on the Web that will be available to all of the students in your class. You can organize similar targeted discussions at any point in a course.

• Consider the demands of online discussions in light of students' workload and time commitments. Balance any required participation with reduced demands in other areas of the course. Otherwise, you can expect students to be reluctant or resentful of the new tasks.

• Require or reward participation to prevent your online discussions from suffering the "empty restaurant syndrome" (the aura of failure that surrounds any place or project that attracts few visitors) or becoming the preserve of a small group of computer enthusiasts. Without clear guidance from the instructor about the importance of this activity, even many of your hardest working students will decline to participate. One particularly successful strategy is to assign one or two students in the class to post a discussion question at the beginning of each week, and another student or pair of students to write a response or follow-up message at the end of the week. Integrate online events (student presentations, debates, interaction with outside experts or other classes) into your course schedule.

- Evaluate the skills and habits of your students. Since many students already use e-mail for personal correspondence, e-mail messages about your course have a high chance of being read. Whatever system you use, you can dramatically reduce student confusion (and time-consuming requests for assistance) by distributing a detailed handout describing how students can perform such basic tasks as sending e-mail to your class list, reaching your course Web site, or using a voice mail conferencing system. Providing telephone and in-person access is especially important for students with limited access to computers or Internet outside of class or off campus.

- Republish (with permission from the authors and in edited form) or bring up in class interesting or provocative dialogues on the Web page or through class handouts. Having their words taken seriously in this manner will encourage student participation.

- Evaluate accessibility issues carefully. Off-campus, technologically challenged, and physically handicapped students may require special arrangements. Find out what campus resources are available to assist these groups.

Finally, to make these technologies work, you must make regular contributions to the electronic dialogue just as you would to a classroom discussion. Online discussions have to be closely monitored to ensure their intellectual usefulness and to reinforce the importance of etiquette in this relatively unfamiliar terrain. You must participate at least periodically to ensure that students take these virtual conversations seriously. But guard your time. Be careful not to create an online discussion in which every query is directed at you. Your participation is essential, but do not allow yourself to become overwhelmed with electronic communications. Some students now expect their instructors to make themselves available twenty-four hours a day seven days a week. Make it clear from the start that the expectation is unrealistic and unreasonable.

Authentic Student Assignments

Ordinarily, when students write short essays or research papers for a course, they write for an audience of one: the instructor. But teachers who have persuaded students that they are writing for a broader audience (a small group of students, the entire class, or the broader public) have found that students take the work more seriously and devote a great deal more effort to it. Creating a system of online publications for your course, or for your department, can have a positive impact on student engagement with scholarly work. Online publishing also creates opportunities for authentic, realistic collaboration, and for students to take a more direct and responsible role in the learning process than they otherwise might. Electronic publishing also exposes students to the stylistic constraints and opportunities of the new digital media, in effect educating them as consumers of electronic material by asking them to author such material and critique their own products. Already, a considerable portion of this nation's business, scholarly, and personal communication occurs through e-mail, the World Wide Web, and private networks of computers. A number of important periodicals exist primarily or solely online, and many students will spend their careers creating and evaluating electronic information.

The range of electronic publishing techniques you use in your course depends largely on the technical skills, resources, and imagination of you or your class. Students have performed the following with considerable success:

- *Multimedia in-class presentations:* A student uses a presentation program to supplement a standard spoken presentation with images, charts and graphs, or sound.
- *Essays in the form of World Wide Web pages:* While even a traditional text essay might be posted for comment, the best essays will make use of the Web's unique ability to incorporate multimedia elements.
- *Web teaching units for your class or other classes:* Students can become teachers by sharing their research and analysis with the class or with an outside audience (including secondary and primary school classes).

- *Web exhibits:* By emulating the form and rigor of museum and library exhibits, students can produce a classroom and community resource on their topic.
- *Collaborative projects:* All of the above projects lend themselves to collaborative work by groups of students.
- *Classroom archive/library:* Over the years, a digitally savvy course might accumulate an excellent library of student essays, teaching units, exhibits, and dialogues on the course topic, telegraphing to new students that their explorations and research are adding to the collective knowledge that informs the course.

But the promise of electronic publishing is almost evenly matched by its perils. The following steps will help you avoid the most common pitfalls:

- Establish and communicate the pedagogical goals of the assignment. Justify deviation from traditional forms of student work by emphasizing that the innovation will improve the knowledge, skills, or learning experience of the students.
- Make the assignment appropriate to the medium. Most rewarding are assignments that make use of multimedia sources, hyperlinks, and collaboration with resources or people over the Internet. For text-only essays, ensure that a classmate or an outside scholar or peer comments on the published papers.
- Provide appropriate technical and stylistic support. Even if the assignment is voluntary, many students will need help with the new requirements of publishing online or preparing multimedia presentations. Arrange for help from your school's computer department, devote a particular class to a group tutorial, or devote a portion of your office hours to technical assistance. Teaching computing skills in non–computer science classes is a controversial practice; be sure not to allow the style of technology to overwhelm the substance.
- Keep technological hurdles as low as possible. If possible, use Web page templates, simple submission forms from your school's LMS, and any other aid that can keep the focus of the class on the subject matter and not the electronic tools. Keep abreast of the

range of technical skill among your students through classroom and school-wide surveys, or even a show of hands on the first day of class.

- Arrange campus, local, scholarly, or international exposure for your students' work. The publishing aspect of the Web is too often assumed to happen spontaneously. A moderate effort at planning how to distribute and publicize your students' publications can ensure that students feel others have taken their work seriously.

- Integrate and archive student work on the course home page. Many students appreciate contributing to the knowledge of the class and to the learning experience of their peers. A gallery of past student work is also effective advertising of your course to prospective students. Pay careful attention to privacy issues regarding student work; school policy and privacy laws may require pseudonyms and anonymous entries when student work is exposed to an outside audience. Certainly you should never publish anything online without the express permission of the author.

As promising as these new media forms might seem, the lack of clear standards for evaluating this work has sometimes hampered their adoption. Teachers are comfortable guiding and evaluating students on traditional essays and presentations. Multimedia presentations or Web pages require even more explicit guidelines to avoid highly uneven and unpredictable results. Electronic projects should fulfill the assignment, make appropriate use of multimedia material, conform to online style conventions, and respect the diversity and size of their potential audience in addition to meeting the scholarly standards of a traditional essay. It is not an easy task, but it is worth trying to do.

Computer technology is becoming both more useful and more cost effective for many fields of teaching. And yet only you, the teacher, can determine whether these methods are worth the effort and likely to prove effective in the classroom. Whatever you decide, remember that technology complements and supplements, but does not fundamentally alter, the core elements of good teaching.

Afterword Why We Teach

This book has attempted to answer a number of questions about how to teach, on the assumption that its readers are people with enough commitment to the academic life to want to teach well. But almost all teachers ask themselves at some point—even at many points—the question not of how to teach, but why. That is a question every teacher must answer, in some measure, alone. But we offer a few observations, drawn from our own experiences, on this central issue of academic life.

One of the realities of teaching, of course, is that the people who benefit most from what we do—our students—disappear from our lives quickly and usually permanently the moment they graduate (if not before) and give us few opportunities to see how we have affected them. And yet nothing is clearer from the long history of education than that good teachers—like good parents—play an enormously important role in the lives of many of their students; that they do, in fact, change students' lives. One of the rewards of good teaching, therefore, should be the knowledge that we have helped shape the futures of many people, that we have instilled modes of thinking, created intellectual passions, promoted forms of tolerance and understanding, and, of course, increased knowledge. That the beneficiaries of our efforts are often invisible to us in no way reduces the value of what we do.

Teaching has rewards to teachers themselves as well. The community of education and scholarship can be a lonely place at times, and it can seem isolated from the larger world. But the academic life at its best is also a broadening life—a life of constant surprises and continuing intellectual growth; a life that forever expands our knowledge of the world and hence the richness of our experience in living out our lives; a life that gives us the opportunity to convey our own passion for what we know to others in the hope that some of them, at least, will come to share it. The wonder and excitement that we sometimes encounter in our students when we help them discover a new area of knowledge is rewarding to us, in part, because it helps us recapture that same wonder and excitement, which is continually within our grasp if we do not lose the will to find it.

Good teaching, finally, is valuable to society—in ways both obvious and obscure. Everyone agrees that education is important, and that effective teaching is the key to education. Students need many skills and much knowledge to succeed in today's rapidly changing world; there is a direct correlation between a person's level of education and his or her chances of professional and economic success in life. But education has another, less immediately visible, social value. It is a vehicle for creating knowledgeable, aware citizens who are capable of looking critically at the world in which they live and making informed decisions about their lives and the lives of others. Education is a way of keeping alive the true basis of democracy: the ability of people to know enough and understand enough about the great issues of their time to help guide their society into its future. In the discouraging moments that all teachers encounter from time to time, it is worth remembering this great goal—which, when things go well, also becomes the great achievement—of devoting one's life to education.

Appendix A Sample Syllabus

HIS 210 Recent History of the United States
Spring 2008, MWF 10–10:50 a.m., Boyer Hall 205
Prof. Jane Smith
Office: Boyer Hall 225 (486-1263; Janesmith@univ.edu)
Office Hours: MWF 12–1 p.m.

1. *Course Description and Structure:* Recent History of the United
   States since 1865 is an overview of American society from 1865
   through the 1990s. The course will focus on the role of the United
   States in the world; the persistence of issues of gender, race, and
   ethnicity; the development of politics and changes in the political
   behavior of Americans; and the shift from a rural agrarian society
   to an urban industrial society to a suburban postindustrial society.
   We will consider a range of primary documents and historians'
   interpretations while we argue our own conclusions to various
   historical questions. Through this process, we will strengthen the
   skills necessary for analytical and critical reading, writing, and
   thinking. The course will be conducted through a combination of
   interactive lectures, discussions among the class as a whole and in
   small groups, debates, and occasional DVDs.
2. *Required Reading:* Please be prepared to discuss the assignments
   from the following books:
   Mary Beth Norton et. al., *A People and a Nation,* Vol. II, since 1865,
     brief 7th ed. (2007). Study guide: http://college.hmco.com/
     history/us/norton/people_nation_brief/7e/student_home.html.
   Elizabeth Cobbs Hoffman and Jon Gjerde, eds, *Major Problems in
     American History,* Vol. II, since 1865, 2nd ed. (2007)
   Thomas Bell, *Out of This Furn*ace (1941)
   Jeffrey P. Moran, *The Scopes Trial, A Brief History with Documents* (2002)
   Glenn C. Altschuler, *All Shook Up: How Rock 'N' Roll Changed
     America* (2004)
   Tim O'Brien, *If I Die in a Combat Zone* (1975)

3. *Participation and Attendance:* Active and thoughtful participation through discussion in all classes is required. Because participation demands your presence in class, attendance is also required.

4. *Required Paper Assignments:* You are required to write two analytical reading papers, about four pages each, one based on Bell, *Out of This Furnace,* Parts I and II only, and the other on Altschuler, *All Shook Up.* I will supply the questions; the paper does not require any additional research beyond the book. All papers must be typed or word-processed in twelve-point font and double-spaced, with one-inch margins. Each paper must include footnotes or endnotes in a standard citation form. Your paper will be evaluated on the strength of your historical arguments and content, how well you have used the reading material required for the paper, composition (i.e., spelling, grammar, sentence structure), and form (i.e., correct citation). In addition to submitting a hard copy of each paper on its due date, you are also required to upload your paper to Turnitin.com by the paper's syllabus due date.

5. *Required Debate:* Each student is required to participate in one debate during the semester. We will have four debates involving two teams of four to five students per team. Each member of the team will be responsible for preparing a written statement of two pages, and for participating orally in the debate. You will receive two grades: one for your individual written contribution, and one for your team performance.

6. *Required Reading Quizzes:* You are required to complete two twenty-minute, short-answer reading quizzes, one on Moran, *The Scopes Trial,* and the other on O'Brien, *If I Die in a Combat Zone.* Please note that there are no makeups on reading quizzes. If you miss a reading quiz for any reason, you will receive a grade of "0" for that quiz.

7. *Evaluation, Exams, Grades:* The requirements of the course are weighted to arrive at your final course grade. You may earn a total of 1,000 points during the semester:

10% or 100 pts	Active and thoughtful class participation
10% or 100 pts	Debate (average of individual paper and group performance)
15% or 150 pts	Two reading quizzes (average of scores on Moran and O'Brien)

15% or 150 pts   Analytical reading paper on Bell, Parts I and II only
15% or 150 pts   Analytical reading paper on Altschuler
15% or 150 pts   Midterm exam
20% or 200 pts   Final exam

Students will have a choice of identifications and essays on all exams. Do not miss the scheduled exams; a medical emergency verified by a doctor's letter is the only acceptable reason for missing midterm or final exams. Makeup exams will consist of two essays (no choice) and are given only on a case-by-case basis.

8. *Academic Honesty and Plagiarism:* You are expected to be familiar with and abide by the university's policies on academic honesty and plagiarism (see the most recent undergraduate catalog). I expect that you will know the definition of plagiarism. To assist you on determining what is and is not plagiarism, I will distribute guidelines describing correct citation form (footnotes and bibliography) and examples of different types of plagiarism. You may study together for quizzes and exams (indeed, I would encourage you to do so), and you may work together on certain group projects. *All papers and exams, however, are to be written only by you.* You may not share notes, rough drafts, or final papers, unless I give you specific instructions about doing so. You are also responsible for being sure that your work is not plagiarized by others. In addition, exams are to be taken independently of any notes, texts, or assistance from others. Failure to abide by the university policies on academic dishonesty and plagiarism may result in an "F" for the course.

9. *University Procedures for Students with Disabilities:* If you have a documented disability, please see me during the first two weeks of class to determine the accommodations that are necessary.

10. *Weekly Schedule of Topics and Assignments:*

WEEK/DATES	TOPICS AND ASSIGNMENTS
1 Jan 14–18	*Topics:* Course introduction; Reconstruction, 1865–77 *Reading due for Wed:* Norton, Ch 16 *Reading due for Fri: Problems,* Intro and 1–15 (docs only). Be prepared to discuss the successes and failures of Reconstruction.

Appendix B Sample Classroom Activities

Simulation Trial of Karl Marx

(Course: World History since 1500; Time: two fifty-minute periods)

Our class will be conducting a simulated trial of Karl Marx, critic of Western industrialization and coauthor, with Friedrich Engels, of *The Communist Manifesto* (1848). In addition to the role of Karl Marx, the trial will also have prosecution and defense teams of attorneys, and a variety of witnesses (contemporaries of Marx and historians) for both the prosecution and defense. The witnesses will also serve as the jury, and your professor will be the presiding judge. We will follow the format of a traditional trial, including opening statements by both the prosecution and defense, questioning and cross-examination of witnesses, lawyers' closing statements, jury deliberation, and finally, rendering of a verdict. Each individual will play a role, and will write a paper based on his or her character's perspective.

The charges against Karl Marx are as follows:

THROUGH HIS PHILOSOPHY AND WRITINGS, MR. KARL MARX IS
1. undermining the economic stability and progress of industrialization in nineteenth-century England, and
2. disrupting traditional class relations in English society.

Attorneys may decide their own order of witnesses. The prosecution will present its case first. Witnesses for the prosecution will be questioned first by one of the prosecuting attorneys and then cross-examined by one of the defense attorneys. After the prosecution rests its case, the defense will proceed with their witnesses, and the prosecution will have the opportunity to cross-examine each defense witness. Attorneys may object to substantive issues relating to historical content, but not to procedural issues (the procedure of the trial itself). After the defense rests, the witnesses will deliberate as a jury to render a verdict.

Attorneys should note time limits for opening statements and questioning and cross-examining witnesses. Please stay within them or risk being held in contempt of court. The judge will sustain or overrule objections.

1. Prosecution team presents opening statements to jury (two minutes each)
2. Defense team presents opening statements to jury (two minutes each)
3. Questioning and cross-examination of prosecution witnesses (two minutes of questions and cross-examination for each witness)
4. Questioning and cross examination of defense witnesses (two minutes of questions and cross-examination for each witness—additional time for Karl Marx)
5. Prosecution team makes closing statement to jury (two minutes)
6. Defense team makes closing statement to jury (two minutes)
7. Jury deliberates for ten minutes—each member will write his or her verdict and the reason for it on a file card. (The verdict does not need to be unanimous.)
8. Verdict

1. All students should complete the required reading of textbook, primary sources, and excerpts of historians' views.
2. Prosecuting and defense attorneys: Using the information in the reading, think about what each of the witnesses believes about industrialization and its impact on 1) economic progress in England, and 2) class relations in English society. Then think about the charges against Marx, and how you might best prosecute or defend him using these witnesses. Then determine your questions for your witnesses, and think about what points you might raise in your cross-examination. Be sure that you write out specific questions for each of your team's witnesses. (A note about questioning and cross-examination: Generally, attorneys want to give their side's witnesses a chance to explain their answers, but when cross-examining the other side's witnesses, attorneys usually try to limit answers to yes or no.)
3. Witnesses: Using the information in the reading, determine what your character's perspective is on industrialization and its impact on

1) economic progress in England, and 2) class relations in English society. Then, using this knowledge, reach some conclusion about what your character would think about the charges against Marx. You must understand thoroughly the historical perspective of your character in order to answer accurately the questions from both prosecution and defense attorneys during the trial.

SUGGESTIONS FOR RESEARCHING AND WRITING

1. Make use of the required reading to determine your character's perspective or your attorney's questions and arguments. Whether you are an attorney or a witness, you should have thoughtful questions, arguments, and responses based on a careful reading and understanding of the historical material.
2. Most witnesses should play their roles as if they were living at the time we are considering. The only witnesses who have the luxury of hindsight are the historians.
3. While I expect that the prosecuting and defense attorneys will work together though discussion of their questions for witnesses and arguments, I expect that each student's individual paper will be written only by that student with no assistance from anyone else on the prosecution or defense team.
4. Attorneys should speak from note cards rather than reading from papers. Make eye contact with your audience, speak loudly and distinctly, and project your voice. I encourage you to use any visuals (i.e., pictures, charts, graphs) for your team's presentation.

REQUIRED PAPER

Each attorney and witness will submit a three-page paper.

1. Attorneys will submit either an opening or closing statement.
2. Witnesses will submit a summary, from the viewpoint of his or her particular character, of his or her views on the accused and the charges against him.

Karl Marx will submit an explanation of why he is not guilty of the charges against him.

Sample Debate

(Course: United States History since 1865; Time: one fifty-minute period)
Resolution for debate: Resolved that the New Deal was successful in improving the lives of ordinary Americans and giving them a larger voice in American society during the 1930s.

DIRECTIONS

Each team will be assigned to argue either the *affirmative position* (arguing in favor of the resolution) or the *negative position* (arguing against the resolution). Your team should gather evidence from the relevant reading and construct logical and sound arguments in defense of your position. Each member of a team will prepare one of the following debate positions in about three pages.

1. Opening Statement (3 minutes): an overview of the issues and a summary of the major points that will be made to defend your group's position
2. Argument(s) (3 minutes): a presentation of the arguments that most strongly support your team's position [Note: if an instructor wished to assign two students, this position could be split into First Argument and Second Argument.]
3. Rebuttal (3 minutes): an attack on the arguments that support the opposing team's positions
4. Closing Argument (3 minutes): a final summary of your team's position and an explanation of the reasons for the superiority of your team's position

Your papers will be collected in class on the day of the debate. Be sure that your paper includes footnotes or endnotes for the resources you used.

FORMAT

The affirmative position will offer its opening statement first, and then teams will alternate until both teams have delivered closing arguments. The teams will then have a three-minute break to organize questions for the other team. A ten-minute period of questions and answers will follow, with each team raising at least two questions to the opposing team. The class will then have ten minutes to question debaters on both teams.

Finally, the class will vote by secret ballot on file cards to determine the more persuasive team by majority vote; each vote should be accompanied by a brief explanation of the reasons for voting as you did.

SUGGESTIONS FOR RESEARCHING, WRITING, AND DEBATING

1. Make use of the required reading to arrive at your arguments and determine the arguments that you can anticipate from your opponents. Talk to other teammates to coordinate your arguments.
2. Anticipate the other side's arguments. Remember that the best defense is often a sharp offense! Be sure that you have sufficient evidence to support your positions and to refute your opponent's arguments.
3. While members of each team may work together though discussion of their arguments and the arguments of the opposition, I expect that each student's individual paper will be written only by that student with no assistance from anyone else on the team.

EVALUATION

You will receive two grades: one for your individual written contribution, and one for your team performance.

Appendix C
Sample Materials for Student Writing Assignments

Grading Rubric

<small>THE "A" CATEGORY</small>

1. *Thesis:* Answers the question clearly with some creativity and/or originality.
2. *Structure:* Has strong transitions and topic sentences that always relate directly to the thesis.
3. *Evidence:* Includes appropriate and persuasive examples at all points.
4. *Analysis:* Always relates evidence directly to the thesis or topic sentence.
5. *Logic:* Presents a strong and balanced argument that refutes opposing viewpoints.
6. *Style:* Contains correct grammar, punctuation, and citation; has appropriate sentence variety and almost no errors.

<small>THE "B" CATEGORY</small>

1. *Thesis:* Answers the question clearly.
2. *Structure:* Has good transitions and topic sentences that usually relate directly to the thesis.
3. *Evidence:* Includes appropriate and persuasive examples at most points.
4. *Analysis:* Often relates evidence directly to the thesis or topic sentence.
5. *Logic:* Presents a good and balanced argument that addresses opposing viewpoints.
6. *Style:* Contains correct grammar, punctuation, and citation; lacks sentence variety and has minor errors.

<small>THE "C" CATEGORY</small>

1. *Thesis:* Answers the question somewhat clearly.
2. *Structure:* Has adequate transitions and topic sentences that sometimes relate to the thesis.

3. *Evidence:* Includes appropriate and persuasive examples at some points.
4. *Analysis:* Sometimes relates evidence directly to the thesis or topic sentence.
5. *Logic:* Presents a coherent but unbalanced argument.
6. *Style:* Contains either numerous minor errors or several major errors in grammar, punctuation, and citation.

THE "D" CATEGORY

1. *Thesis:* Fails to answer the question clearly.
2. *Structure:* Has weak transitions and few topic sentences that relate directly to the thesis.
3. *Evidence:* Includes few appropriate or persuasive examples.
4. *Analysis:* Rarely relates evidence directly to the thesis or topic sentence.
5. *Logic:* Presents an incoherent and unbalanced argument.
6. *Style:* Contains major and frequent errors in grammar, punctuation, and citation.

THE "F" CATEGORY

The paper reflects minimal effort and/or minimal comprehension of the assignment.

Paper Checklist

Please complete the following checklist and include it with the final draft of your paper.

STRUCTURE

( ) 1. I have created an introductory paragraph that provides appropriate background or captures the reader's interest with a dramatic incident or colorful anecdote.
( ) 2. I have created a thesis paragraph that introduces the argument clearly and thoroughly. It also defines key terms I will use in my paper.
( ) 3. I have created a "roadmap" paragraph that outlines the major sections and, if appropriate, introduces the main works consulted.
( ) 4. I have created a conclusion that restates and extends the argument. It also brings the paper to a memorable finish.

( ) 5. I have thought about how my paragraphs are arranged and have structured them in a way that best supports my argument.

( ) 6. I have confirmed that each paragraph has a topic sentence and that they flow logically from the preceding paragraph.

SUBSTANCE

( ) 1. I have developed a clear argument.

( ) 2. I have developed a creative argument.

( ) 3. I have used appropriate evidence from multiple sources in support of the argument.

( ) 4. I have analyzed the relative validity and credibility of different sources.

( ) 5. I have presented contradictory arguments and addressed them fairly and carefully through concession or refutation.

( ) 6. I have verified that each paragraph contains evidence to support the topic sentence and the overall argument of the paper.

STYLE

( ) 1. I have proofread the paper for spelling, punctuation, citation, and grammar errors.

( ) 2. I have read the paper aloud to myself or to someone else, listening for sentences that do not make sense or seem too long.

( ) 3. I have had a friend or classmate check the paper for some or all of the problems identified in the style sheet.

( ) 4. I have followed the grammar guidelines in the style sheet.

( ) 5. I have followed the policies on quotation usage in the style sheet.

( ) 6. I have followed the format standards in the style sheet.

Style Sheet

SUGGESTIONS (S)

1. Avoid the passive voice, as in "The bill was passed by Congress." Make it active by identifying the subject of the sentence and placing it before the verb. For example, "Congress passed the bill." The active voice will make your writing more energetic and engaging.

2. Keep verb tenses consistent and use the tense that is appropriate to the context. When talking about historical events, use past tense.

When talking about current events, use present tense. If you use present tense when referring to source material (e.g., In *On the Origin of Species,* Darwin writes . . .), do so consistently throughout your paper.

3. Divide your essay into distinct paragraphs, usually consisting of four to six sentences. Organize each paragraph around a main idea, expressed in a topic sentence that typically comes at the start. In the remainder of the paragraph, elaborate upon the idea or provide supporting material in the form of specific evidence or logical reasoning.

4. Words to use with care: it's and its; affect and effect; lead and led; fewer and less.

5. Words to avoid: very; basically; clearly; interestingly; feel; therefore.

6. Fully identify a person upon first mention. For example, first introduce the commander of D-Day as "Dwight D. Eisenhower, the Supreme Allied Commander in Europe." Then refer to him subsequently as "Eisenhower" only. No first names after the initial mention please—alone especially.

7. Try to avoid the use of "there is" or "there were." For example, rewrite "there were many factors behind Joseph Stalin's rise to power" as "many factors contributed to Joseph Stalin's rise to power."

8. Use exclamation marks and italics for emphasis only—and then sparingly.

GRAMMAR AND PUNCTUATION (G&P)

1. Watch for noun-verb agreement. If the subject is plural, then related pronouns and the verb must be in plural form also. Students prepare themselves, not himself or herself.

2. When referring back to a person, use "who" not "that" as in "Tom, who wanted to see a movie, instead went to dinner with friends."

3. A comma can be used to set off phrases or clauses or to separate items in a series. It can be used to join two sentences only when it is used with a conjunction.

4. A semicolon can be used to join two otherwise complete sentences.

5. A colon can be used to introduce a list of items or an illustrative quotation. It can also be used to join two closely related complete

sentences when the second one elaborates on or clarifies the
first one.

QUOTATIONS (Q)

1. *A sentence can never consist entirely of a quotation.*
2. Punctuation: Periods and commas always fall within the last
   quotation mark while semicolons generally come after it. Question
   and exclamation marks should be inside the quotation marks if they
   are part of the original quote, and outside the quotation marks if they
   are part of your sentence.
3. Always provide context for the quotation. Introduce it so that the
   reader knows what is coming. Offer analysis of the quotation after it
   has appeared so that the reader understands both its significance and
   its relation to the thesis or topic sentence.
4. Do not correct the spelling or grammar within a quotation. If an
   author has italicized part of the quotation for emphasis, do not
   reproduce the italics in your paper. Add words within brackets ("[ ]")
   if it is necessary to make the meaning clear—but do so sparingly
   and carefully. You may change the first capital letter of a sentence
   into a lowercase letter to merge the quotation into one of your
   sentences.
5. Reread all sentences with quoted material several times. Make sure
   they remain grammatically correct. As a test, remove the quotation
   marks. Does the sentence now pass the grammar test? If not,
   rewrite it.
6. Avoid lengthy quotations. Try not to include more than one sentence
   within a set of quotation marks. If you must use a "block" quotation,
   it should be indented and single-spaced without quotation marks.
   Add one line space both before and after the "block" quotation.
7. Use ellipses (". . .") to eliminate superfluous material within a
   quotation. But make sure that you do not alter the meaning of the
   material.
8. Try to quote from primary sources and always provide a footnote or
   endnote. Try to paraphrase material from secondary sources, unless
   they are exceptionally eloquent. No more than 20 percent of your
   paper should consist of quoted material. Increase the impact of the

quotations you select by employing fewer of them. Remember that less is often more.

FORMAT (F)

1. *Title page:* Include the title of the paper, your name, my name, the course number or title, and the date. Do not repeat this information on the first page of your paper.
2. *Bibliography:* Begin on a new page labeled Bibliography or Works Consulted at the top. Bibliographic citations should conform to the style outlined in Turabian or whatever style manual you use. The bibliography should include all works consulted, not merely those cited.
3. *Line spacing:* Double-space the text of your paper (unless you have included a block quotation). Single-space the footnotes or endnotes—but place an extra line between them.
4. *Page numbers:* Number each page. Omit the number from the first page or the title page.
5. *Margins:* Use one-inch margins for the sides, top, and bottom of your paper.
6. *Typeface:* For the typeface, use a simple font like Courier or Times New Roman. Clarity and ease of reading are the goals; avoid fancy but difficult-to-read fonts.

Appendix D Sample Exam

The exam contains three sections. The recommended time indicates the relative value. Please follow the directions carefully and spend your time accordingly.

Part I: Identification (20 minutes)

Choose THREE. In a substantial paragraph, identify the name or term (who, what, where, when) AND explain why it was important to recent U.S. history.

Michael Harrington	Vienna Summit
Cesar Chavez	Head Start
Helen Gurley Brown	*Milliken v. Bradley*

Part II: Analysis (20 minutes)

Analyze ONE of the excerpts in a brief essay (five paragraphs). First, place the source in historical context. Second, identify the author and explain his or her motives. Third, discuss the argument the source as a whole presents. Fourth, consider the audience(s) for the source. Finally, assess the historical significance of the source.

> "We are people of this generation, bred in at least modest comfort, housed now in universities, looking uncomfortably to the world we inherit. . . . As a social system we seek the establishment of a democracy of individual participation, governed by two central aims: that the individual share in those social decisions determining the quality and direction of his life; that society be organized to encourage independence in men and provide the media for their common participation."

> "The economic ills we suffer have come upon us over several decades. They will not go away in days, weeks, or months, but they will go away. They will go away because we as Americans have the capacity now, as we've had in the past, to do whatever needs to be done to preserve this last and greatest bastion of freedom. In this

present crisis, government is not the solution to our problem; government is the problem."

Part III: Chronology (20 minutes)

Select ONE of the "clusters." In a brief essay (five paragraphs), place the events in chronological order AND explain their causal relationship.

Civil Rights Act introduced in Congress; President Kennedy assassinated; Birmingham demonstrations; March on Washington; Civil Rights Act signed into law

President Johnson announces that he will not run for reelection; antiwar protests erupt at the Democratic Convention in Chicago; Tet Offensive begins; Robert Kennedy enters the presidential race; Eugene McCarthy "wins" the New Hampshire Democratic primary

Appendix E Sample Concept Map

Sexual Dimorphism Concept Map
(Dr. Sarah Leupen of Ohio Wesleyan University provided this activity.)

INSTRUCTIONS FOR STUDENTS

In your envelope are nine slips of paper, each naming a sexual dimorphism (difference between male and female animals) that applies to most or all animals. Your job is to arrange these dimorphisms in a way that reflects your hypotheses about their causal relationships, and thus their likely evolutionary relationship. You can connect your slips of paper with arrows or linking phrases. For example, if you had a slip of paper that said "only male animals sing to attract mates," you could put an arrow leading to this from "males usually compete for females rather than vice versa," since we believe that the reason males sing directly follows from the fact that they face more competition for mates.

To begin, it is easiest to start with the *most fundamental* difference between male and female animals and work "forward" from there. Your map will probably branch and perhaps even circle, rather than be a single line. There is no correct answer here, but you should be prepared to defend each of your connections.

INSTRUCTIONS FOR TEACHERS

1. Divide the students into groups of two to four and give each group a copy of the above directions, a large (11" × 17") sheet of paper, a small roll of tape, and an envelope with nine slips of paper containing the statements below (preferably printed in large, twenty-four point type, although you could also have the students write the slips themselves to save time).
2. While the students make the maps, circulate in the classroom, answering questions and probing for the logic behind the student arrangements.
3. After fifteen minutes or whenever the groups have finished, ask two or three groups to present and explain their concept maps to

the class. Have the other groups offer comments and compare the results.

SEXUAL DIMORPHISMS

Sperm are smaller than eggs

Females (not males) have uteruses

Males have more to gain from having multiple mates

Males usually compete for females rather than vice versa

The brightly colored sex is usually the male

Males (not females) have penises

Males make more gametes (sperm) than females do (eggs)

Testes are bigger than ovaries

Females provide most or all parental care

Appendix F Sample Evaluations

Below are some sample evaluation forms designed for various purposes. Your own course will undoubtedly have special needs of its own, but you may wish to use one of the following forms as a starting point for your own.

For a graduate student leading a discussion section; to be administered during the first several weeks of class.

> Please circle the number that is most appropriate and write answers to the other questions.
>
> 1. Do you find discussion sections helpful?
>   Very helpful   7 6 5 4 3 2 1   Not helpful
>
> 2. What might be improved about the section?
>
> 3. How would you rate the instructor on the following?
>   a. Approachability? 7 6 5 4 3 2 1
>   b. As a facilitator of discussion? 7 6 5 4 3 2 1
>   c. Knowledge of subject? 7 6 5 4 3 2 1
>   d. As an evaluator of your work? 7 6 5 4 3 2 1
>   e. What suggestions can you make for improvement
>   of the items above?
>
> 4. Is there any topic or activity not presently included in the section that should be added? Why?
>
> 5. Is there any topic or activity that should be omitted? Why?
>
> 6. Feel free to make any additional comments about the class.
>
> Thanks for taking the time to complete this form!

For an instructor during the first several weeks of the term.

Please answer the following questions concerning the course. Fill in the blank space with the appropriate number ranking from most effective to least effective. Do not write your name on this form.

Circle your student status:
Freshman   Sophomore   Junior   Senior   Graduate

Most Effective			Average		Least Effective	
7	6	5	4	3	2	1

1. Are the course objectives clear? _____
2. Are the lectures clear and organized? _____
3. Is the reading useful? _____
4. Are discussions helpful? _____
5. Are the writing assignments useful? _____
6. Does the classroom atmosphere facilitate your learning? _____
7. Is the instructor accessible outside of the classroom? _____

Please evaluate each of the books we are reading: [List them.]

Comment on any aspect of the course, particularly lectures, required reading, and writing assignments, and offer suggestions on how the course might be improved. Thank you for your time.

For an instructor at the end of a course. These are sample questions that might be used to elicit narrative responses, or they could be adapted for a quantitative rating.

Evaluate yourself as a student in this course.
1. How much effort and preparation did you put into each class?
2. What do you think is your role as a student in the course?

Evaluate the performance of the instructor.
1. Does the teacher appear enthusiastic about the class?
2. Are lectures organized and presented clearly?
3. Are deadlines and responsibilities reasonable?
4. Are papers and exams returned to students in a reasonable amount of time?
5. Are comments on exams and papers instructive?
6. Is the instructor available outside of class?
7. Are office hours sufficient? Are they conveniently scheduled?

Evaluate the course content and reading.
1. Is the required reading useful for gaining an understanding of the course content?
2. Are the course themes clear?
3. What topics do you like the most and why?
4. What topics do you like the least and why?

Evaluate instructional methods.
1. How useful is each of the following methods used in the class: lecture, discussion, collaborative learning through groups, debates, simulations, oral presentations, videos. [List methods separately so students can comment on each.]
2. Do you have a reasonable amount of class time to ask questions?
3. Do the assignments help you to understand the subject?

Please suggest other teaching techniques that might be used in this class. Be as specific as possible.

Suggestions for Further Reading

General Works

Baicco, Sharon A., and Jamie N. Dewaters. *Successful College Teaching: Problem-Solving Strategies of Distinguished Professors*. Boston: Allyn and Bacon, 1998.

Bain, Ken. *What the Best College Teachers Do*. Cambridge, MA: Harvard University Press, 2004.

Banner, James M., Jr., and Harold C. Cannon. *The Elements of Teaching*. New Haven, CT: Yale University Press, 1997.

Boyle, Eleanor, and Harley Rothstein. *Essentials of College and University Teaching: A Practical Guide*. Stillwater, OK: New Forums Press, 2003.

Campbell, William E., and Karl A. Smith, eds. *New Paradigms for College Teaching*. Edina, MN: Interaction Book Co., 1997.

Chickering, Arthur W., and Selda Gamson, eds. *Applying the Seven Principles for Good Practice in Undergraduate Education*. San Francisco: Jossey-Bass, 1991.

Committee on Undergraduate Science Education. *Science Teaching Reconsidered: A Handbook*. Washington, DC: National Academy Press, 1997.

Davidson, Cliff I., and Susan A. Ambrose. *The New Professor's Handbook: A Guide to Teaching and Research in Engineering and Science*. Bolton, MA: Anker Publishing Co., 1994.

Davis, Barbara Gross. *Tools for Teaching*. San Francisco: Jossey-Bass, 1993.

Eble, Kenneth E. *The Craft of Teaching: A Guide to Mastering the Professor's Art*. San Francisco: Jossey-Bass, 1988.

Fenstermacher, Gary D., and Jonas F. Soltis. *Approaches to Teaching*. New York: Teachers College Press, 1992.

Filene, Peter. *The Joy of Teaching: A Practical Guide for New College Instructors*. Chapel Hill: University of North Carolina Press, 2005.

Fried, Robert L., and Deborah Meier. *The Passionate Teacher*. Boston: Beacon Press, 1996.

Fuhrmann, Barbara Schneider, and Anthony F. Grasha. *A Practical Handbook for College Teachers*. Boston: Little, Brown and Co., 1983.

Gibson, Gerald W. *Good Start: A Guidebook for New Faculty in Liberal Arts Colleges*. Bolton, MA: Anker Publishing Co., 1992.

Gullette, Margaret Morganroth, ed. *The Art and Craft of Teaching*. Cambridge, MA: Harvard University Press, 1984.

Highet, Gilbert. *The Art of Teaching*. New York: Vintage Books, 1989.

Hodge, Bonnie M., and Jennie Preston-Sabin, eds. *Accommodations—or Just Good Teaching? Strategies for Teaching College Students with Disabilities.* Westport, CT: Praeger, 1997.

Lang, James M. *On Course: A Week-by-Week Guide to Your First Semester of College Teaching.* Cambridge, MA: Harvard University Press, 2008.

Lowman, Joseph. *Mastering the Techniques of Teaching.* San Francisco: Jossey-Bass, 1984.

Magnan, Robert, ed. *147 Practical Tips for Teaching Professors.* Madison, WI: Magna Publications, 1990.

McGlynn, Angela Provitera. *Successful Beginnings for College Teachers.* Madison, WI: Atwood Publishing, 2001.

McKeachie, Wilbert J. *McKeachie's Teaching Tips: Strategies, Research, and Theory for College and University Teachers.* 11th ed. Boston: Houghton Mifflin Co., 2002.

Royse, David. *Teaching Tips for College and University Instructors.* Needham Heights, MA: Allyn and Bacon, 2001.

Sawyer, R. McLaran, et al., eds. *The Art and Politics of College Teaching: A Practical Guide for the Beginning Professor.* New York: Peter Lang Publishing, 1992.

Stocking, S. Holly, et al. *More Quick Hits: Successful Strategies by Award-Winning Teachers.* Bloomington: Indiana University Press, 1998.

Weimer, Maryellen, and Rose Ann Neff, eds. *Teaching College: Collected Readings for the New Instructor.* Madison, WI: Atwood Publishing, 1998.

1 Getting Ready

"Effective Course Materials," "Selecting a Textbook," "Course Materials Review." *Teaching Professor* 1, no. 6 (August 1987): 1–4.

Flamm, Michael W. "Power Point: The Promise and Pitfalls." *American Historical Association Perspectives* 46, no. 3 (March 2008): 26–27.

O'Brien, Judith Grunert, et al. *The Course Syllabus: A Learning-Centered Approach.* 2nd ed. San Francisco: Jossey-Bass, 2008.

Slattery, Jeanne M., and Janet F. Carlson. "Preparing an Effective Syllabus: Current Best Practices." *College Teaching,* 53, no. 4 (Fall 2005): 159–64.

Wasley, Paula. "The Syllabus Becomes a Repository of Legalese." *Chronicle of Higher Education* 54, no. 27 (March 2008): 1.

2 The First Weeks

Dorn, Dean S. "The First Day of Class: Problems and Strategies." *Teaching Sociology* 15, no. 1 (January 1987): 61–72.

"The First Day of Class: Advice and Ideas." *Teaching Professor* 3, no. 7 (1989): 1–2.

Fraher, Richard. "Learning a New Art: Suggestions for Beginning Teachers."
    Chap. 9 in *The Art and Craft of Teaching,* edited by Margaret Morganroth
    Gullette. Cambridge, MA: Harvard University Press, 1984.
Nash, Laura L. "The Rhythms of the Semester." Chap. 6 in *The Art and Craft
    of Teaching,* ed. Margaret Morganroth Gullette. Cambridge, MA: Harvard
    University Press, 1984.
"What to Do on the First Day of Class (The Round Table)." *English Journal* 77, no.
    5 (September 1988): 89–91.

3 Active and Collaborative Learning

Barkley, Elizabeth, et al. *Collaborative Learning Techniques: A Handbook for College
    Faculty.* San Francisco: Jossey-Bass, 2004
Blumberg, Phyllis. *Developing Learner-Centered Teaching: A Practical Guide for
    Faculty.* San Francisco: Jossey-Bass, 2008.
Bowers, C. A., and David J. Flinders. *Responsive Teaching: An Ecological Approach
    to Classroom Patterns of Language, Culture, and Thought.* New York: Teachers
    College Press, 1990.
Brockbank, Anne, and Ian McGill. *Facilitating Reflective Learning in Higher
    Education.* 2nd ed. Philadelphia: Society for Research into Higher Education
    and Open University Press, 2007.
Brookfield, Stephen D., and Stephen Preskill. *Discussion as a Way of Teaching:
    Tools and Techniques for Democratic Classrooms.* 2nd ed. San Francisco: Jossey-
    Bass, 2005.
Edwards, Clifford H. *Classroom Discipline and Management.* 5th ed. Hoboken, NJ:
    Wiley Blackwell, 2007.
Frederick, Peter. "The Dreaded Discussion: Ten Ways to Start." *Improving College
    and University Teaching* 29, no. 3 (Summer 1981): 109–14.
Rabow, Jerome, et al. *William Fawcett Hills' Learning through Discussion.* 3rd ed.
    Long Grove, IL: Waveland Press, 1994.
"Student Recommendations for Encouraging Participation." *Teaching Professor* 19,
    no. 1 (January 2005): 4–5.
Vredenburg, Debra. "Using On-Line Discussion Forums for Minute Papers."
    Teaching Professor 18, no. 10 (December 2004): 6.

4 The Art and Craft of Lecturing

Alexander, James D. "Lectures: The Ethics of Borrowing." *College Teaching* 36, no.
    1 (Winter 1988): 20–24.
Blackey, Robert. "New Wine in Old Bottles: Revitalizing the Traditional History
    Lecture." *Teaching History* 22, no. 1 (Spring 1997): 3–25.

Frederick, Peter J. "The Lively Lecture—Eight Variations." *College Teaching* 34, no. 2 (Spring 1986): 43–50.

Geske, J. "Overcoming the Drawbacks of the Large Lecture Class." *College Teaching* 40, no. 4 (1992): 151–54.

Gullette, Margaret Morganroth. "Leading Discussion in a Lecture Course: Some Maxims and an Exhortation." *Change* 24, no. 2 (March/April 1992): 32–39.

Penner, Jon G. *Why Many College Teachers Cannot Lecture: How to Avoid Communication Breakdown in the Classroom.* Springfield, IL: Charles C. Thomas, 1984.

Sitler, Helen Collins. "The Spaced Lecture." *College Teaching* 45, no. 3 (Summer 1997): 108–10.

Weimer, Maryellen Gleason, ed. *Teaching Large Classes Well: New Directions for Teaching and Learning,* no. 32. San Francisco: Jossey-Bass, Winter 1992.

5 Student Writing and Research

"Make the Most of Written Feedback." *Teaching Professor* 5, no. 7 (1991): 1–2.

Malehorn, H. "Term Papers for Sale and What to Do about It." *Improving College and University Teaching* 31, no. 3 (1983): 107–8.

Simon, L. "The Papers We Want to Read." *College Teaching* 36, no. 1 (1988): 6–8.

Walvoord, B. F. *Helping Students Write Well: A Guide for Teachers in All Disciplines.* 2nd ed. New York: Modern Language Association, 1986.

Walvoord, B. F., and Virginia Johnson Anderson. *Effective Grading: A Tool for Learning and Assessment.* San Francisco: Jossey-Bass, 1998.

6 Testing and Evaluation

Angelo, Thomas A., and Kathryn P. Cross. *Classroom Assessment Techniques: A Handbook for College Teachers.* 2nd ed. San Francisco: Jossey-Bass, 1993.

Blackey, Robert, ed. *History Anew: Innovations in the Teaching of History Today.* Long Beach: University Press of California State University, 1993.

"Exams: Alternative Ideas and Approaches." *Teaching Professor* 3, no. 8 (1990): 3–4.

Jacobs, L. C., and C. I. Chase. *Developing and Using Tests Effectively: A Guide for Faculty.* San Francisco: Jossey-Bass, 1992.

Murray, John P. "Better Testing for Better Learning." *College Teaching* 38, no. 4 (Fall 1990): 148–52.

7 Teaching Science: Challenges and Approaches

Cavallo, A. M. L., M. Rozman, J. Blinkenstaf, and N. Walker. "Students' Learning Approaches, Reasoning Abilities, Motivation Goals and Epistemological Beliefs." *Journal of College Science Teaching* 33 (2003): 18–23.

Herreid, C. F. "Case Studies in Science—a Novel Method for Science Education." *Journal of College Science Teaching* 23 (1994): 221–29.

Mintzes, Joel J., and William H. Leonard, eds., *Handbook of College Science Teaching*. Arlington, VA: National Science Teachers Association Press, 2006.

"Promoting Active Learning in the Life Science Classroom." In *Annals of the New York Academy of Sciences,* edited by Harold I. Modell, Joel A. Michael, Robert G. Carroll, and Daniel Richardson. Wiley-Blackwell, 1993.

Sunderberg, M. D., J. E. Armstrong, M. Dini, and W. Wischusen. "Some Practical Tips for Instituting Investigative Biology Laboratories. *Journal of College Science Teaching* 29 (2000): 353–59.

Zusho, A., and P. R. Pintrich. "Skill and Will: The Role of Motivation and Cognition in the Learning of College Chemistry." *International Journal of Science Education* 25 (2003): 1081–94.

8 Evaluating Your Teaching

Doyle, Kenneth O. *Student Evaluation of Instruction*. Lexington, MA: Lexington Books (D. C. Heath), 1975.

Eble, Kenneth E. *The Recognition and Evaluation of Teaching*. Salt Lake City: Project to Improve College Teaching, 1970.

England, James, Pat Hutchings, and Wilbert J. McKeachie. *The Professional Evaluation of Teaching*. New York: American Council of Learned Societies, 1996.

Krupnick, Catherine G. "The Uses of Videotape Replay." In *Teaching and the Case Method: Text, Cases, and Readings,* edited by C. Roland Christensen with Abby J. Hansen, 256–63. Boston: Harvard Business School, 1987.

"Teaching Journals: A Self-Evaluation Strategy." *Teaching Professor* 2, no. 6 (June 1988): 2.

Weimer, Maryellen. *Improving College Teaching: Strategies for Developing Instructional Effectiveness*. San Francisco: Jossey-Bass, 1990.

9 Teaching as a Part-Time Instructor

Chism, Nancy Van Note, ed. *Faculty at the Margins: New Directions for Higher Education, No. 143*. San Francisco: Jossey-Bass, 2008.

Dessants, Betty A. "Teaching and the Job Interview." In *Perspectives on Life after a History Ph. D.,* edited by Richard Bond and Pillarisetti Sudhir. Washington, DC: American Historical Association, 2005.

"Four Types of Unethical Behavior To Avoid." *Teaching Professor* 18, no. 4 (April 2004): 4–6.

Keith-Spiegel, Patricia, et al. *The Ethics of Teaching: A Casebook*. 2nd ed. Psychology Press (Routledge), 2002.

Lambert, Leo, Stacey Lane Tice, and Patricia H. Featherstone, eds. *University Teaching: A Guide for Graduate Students*. Syracuse, NY: Syracuse University Press, 1996.

Lyons, Richard E. *Success Strategies for Adjunct Faculty*. Upper Saddle River, NJ: Allyn and Bacon, 2003.

Nyquist, Jody D., and Donald H. Wulff. *Working Effectively with Graduate Assistants*. Thousand Oaks, CA: Sage Publications, 1996.

Schneider, Beth E. "Graduate Women, Sexual Harassment, and University Policy." *Journal of Higher Education* 58, no. 1 (January/February 1987): 46–65.

Segerstrale, Ullica. "The Multifaceted Role of the Section Leader." Chap. 5 in *The Art and Craft of Teaching*, edited by Margaret Morganroth Gullette. Cambridge, MA: Harvard University Press, 1984.

Seldin, Peter, and J. Elizabeth Miller. *The Teaching Portfolio: A Practical Guide to Documenting Teaching, Research and Service*. San Francisco: Jossey-Bass, 2008.

10 Creating and Sustaining an Inclusive Classroom

Adams, Maurianne, Lee Anne Bell, and Pat Griffin, eds. *Teaching for Diversity and Social Justice*. 2nd ed. New York: Routledge, 2007.

Brookfield, Stephen. *Becoming a Critically Reflective Teacher*. San Francisco: Jossey-Bass, 1995.

Burgsthaler, Sheryl E., and Rebecca C. Coy. *Universal Design in Higher Education: From Principles to Practice*. Cambridge: MA. Harvard Education Press, 2008.

Tuitt, Frank. "Afterword: Realizing a More Inclusive Pedagogy." In *Race and Higher Education: Rethinking Pedagogy in Diverse College Classrooms*, edited by Annie Howell and Frank Tuitt, 129–38. Cambridge, MA: Harvard Education Publishing Group, 2003.

Warren, Lee. "Strategic Action in Hot Moments." In *Teaching Inclusively: Resources for Course, Department and Institutional Change in Higher Education*, edited by Mathew L. Ouellett, 620–30. Stillwater, OK: New Forums, 2005.

11 Using Electronic Resources in Teaching

Bates, Tony, and Gary Poole. *Effective Teaching with Technology in Higher Education: Foundations for Success*. 1st ed. Jossey-Bass Higher and Adult Education Series. San Francisco: Jossey-Bass, 2003.

Beetham, Helen, and Rhona Sharpe. *Rethinking Pedagogy for a Digital Age: Designing and Delivering E-Learning*. New York, NY: Routledge, 2007.

Boschmann, Erwin. *The Electronic Classroom: A Handbook for Education in the Electronic Environment*. Medford, NJ: Learned Information, 1995.

John, Peter D., and Steve Wheeler. *The Digital Classroom: Harnessing Technology for the Future of Learning and Teaching*. London; New York: Routledge, 2008.

Laurillard, Diana. *Rethinking University Teaching: A Conversational Framework for the Effective Use of Learning Technologies.* 2nd ed. London; New York: RoutledgeFalmer, 2002.

Oblinger, Diana, and James L. Oblinger. *Educating the Net Generation.* Boulder, CO: EDUCAUSE, 2005. http://bibpurl.oclc.org/web/9463.

Palloff, Rena M., and Keith Pratt. *Building Online Learning Communities: Effective Strategies for the Virtual Classroom.* 2nd ed. Jossey-Bass Higher and Adult Education Series. San Francisco: Jossey-Bass, 2007.

Poole, Bernard John. *Education for an Information Age: Teaching in the Computerized Classroom.* 2nd ed. Boston: WCB/McGraw Hill, 1997.

Sandholtz, Judith Haymore, Cathy Ringstaff, and David C. Dwyer. *Teaching with Technology: Creating Student-Centered Classrooms.* New York: Teachers College Press, 1997.

Tuman, Myron C. *Literacy Online: The Promise (and Peril) of Reading and Writing with Computers.* Pittsburgh Series in Composition, Literacy, and Culture. Pittsburgh: University of Pittsburgh Press, 1992.

About the Authors

Alan Brinkley is the Allan Nevins Professor of History and former provost at Columbia University. Among his publications are *Voices of Protest: Huey Long, Father Coughlin, and the Great Depression* (which won the National Book Award); *The End of Reform: New Deal Liberalism in Recession and War; Liberalism and Its Discontents; Franklin Delano Roosevelt; The Publisher: Henry Luce and His American Century;* and two college textbooks, *American History: A Survey* and *The Unfinished Nation: A Concise History of the American People.* He was awarded the Joseph Levenson Teaching Award at Harvard and the Great Teacher Award at Columbia.

Betty Dessants is associate professor of history at Shippensburg University where she specializes in twentieth-century U.S. history, particularly Cold War foreign relations and society. She has published in the areas of World War II and Cold War intelligence, Cold War culture, and college teaching. Prior to teaching at the university level, she taught history in secondary public and independent schools. She has given numerous presentations on the craft of teaching.

Esam El-Fakahany is professor of psychiatry, pharmacology, and neuroscience at the University of Minnesota Medical School. He is also former associate dean of the Graduate School. He cofounded and directed the University of Minnesota's first office for postdoctoral affairs. He is coauthor of *The Chicago Guide to Your Career in Science.*

Michael Flamm is professor of history at Ohio Wesleyan University, where he was awarded the Bishop Francis Emner Kearns Teacher of the Year Award. He leads workshops and seminars on behalf of the Gilder Lehrman Institute of American History, and taught previously at public high schools in New Jersey and New York. He has also taught at San Andrés University in Buenos Aires as a Fulbright Senior Specialist. He is the author or coauthor of five books, including *Law and Order: Street Crime, Civil Unrest, and the Crisis of Liberalism in the 1960s; Debating the Reagan Presidency;* and *Debating the 1960s: Liberal, Conservative, and Radical Perspectives.*

Charles B. Forcey, Jr., is a Ph.D. candidate in modern American intellectual history at Columbia University. He has been an instructor at Columbia and the University of New Hampshire. He is presently founder and owner of Historicus, Inc., a firm dedicated to the effective use of technology in humanities teaching, research, and publishing. His projects include the Primary Source Investigator for McGraw-Hill, a series of political science simulations for Cengage Learning, and a wide variety of museum- and university-based exhibits and teaching projects.

Mathew L. Ouellett is director of the Center for Teaching at the University of Massachusetts Amherst, where he works with faculty and teaching assistants on a full complement of teaching and learning development initiatives. He also teaches in the Higher Education program at the University of Massachusetts Amherst as well as in the Smith College School of Social Work. He edited the volume *Teaching Inclusively: Resources for Course, Departmental and Institutional Change in Higher Education* (New Forums Press, 2005), and contributed two chapters to *A Guide to Faculty Development: Practical Advice, Examples, and Resources* (Jossey-Bass, forthcoming).

Eric Rothschild is a history teacher who retired in 1998 as chair of the Social Studies Department at Scarsdale High School after thirty-six years in the classroom. He has also taught at Manhattan College and LaSalle University. He was New York State Social Studies Educator of the Year in 1991 and served on the executive board of the Organization of American History from 1991 to 1994. He has written extensively on advanced placement and on simulations and is the author of *The New York Times School Microfilm Collection*.

Index